Practice Papers for SQA Exams

Standard Grade | General/Credit

English

ISBN 978-1-84372-768-2

Published by
Leckie & Leckie Ltd, 3rd floor, 4 Queen Street, Edinburgh, EH2 1JE
Tel: 0131 220 6831 Fax: 0131 225 9987
enquiries@leckieandleckie.co.uk   www.leckieandleckie.co.uk

A CIP Catalogue record for this book is available from the British Library.

Leckie & Leckie Ltd is a division of Huveaux plc.

Questions and answers in this book do not emanate from SQA. All of our entirely new and original Practice Papers have been written by experienced authors working directly for the publisher

Text acknowledgements
The following company has very generously given permission to reproduce their copyright material free of charge:
The Barn Owl Trust (General Reading exam A)

Leckie & Leckie is grateful to the copyright holders, as credited below, for permission to use their material:
Scotsman Publications Ltd for the article 'Ballad of St Kilda' (Credit Reading exam A)
Extract from 'The Lieutenant' (General Reading exam B) by Kate Grenville, first published in Great Britain by Canongate Books Ltd, 14 High Street, Edinburgh, EH1 1TE
Extract from 'The Star of the Sea' (Credit Reading exam B) by Joseph O'Connor, published by Secker & Warburg/Vintage. Reprinted by permission of the Random House Group Ltd.
Extract from 'Made in America' (General Reading exam C) by Bill Bryson, published by Black Swan. Reprinted by permission of the Random House Group Ltd.
Extract from 'Distant Voices', *The Man with no Name* (Credit Reading exam C) by John Pilger, published by Random House.

Every effort has been made to trace the copyright holders and to obtain their permission for the use of copyright material. Leckie & Leckie will gladly receive information enabling them to rectify any error or omission in subsequent editions.

Photograph acknowledgements
All photographs in FGC Writing exam (pages 59–63) © 2009 Jupiterimages Corporation

Introduction

Layout of the Book

This book contains practice exam papers, which mirror the actual SQA exam as much as possible. The layout, paper colour and question level are all similar to the actual exam that you will sit, so that you are familiar with what the exam paper will look like.

The answer section is at the back of the book. Each answer contains a worked-out answer or solution so that you can see how the right answer has been arrived at. The answers also include practical tips on how to tackle certain types of questions, details of how marks are awarded and advice on just what the examiners will be looking for.

Revision advice is provided in this introductory section of the book, so please read on!

How To Use This Book

The Practice Papers can be used in two main ways:

1. You can complete an entire practice paper as preparation for the final exam. If you would like to use the book in this way, you can complete the practice paper under exam-style conditions by setting yourself a time for each paper and answering it as well as possible without using any references or notes.
    Alternatively, you can answer the practice paper questions as a revision exercise, using your notes to produce a model answer. Your teacher may mark these for you.

2. You can use the Topic Index at the front of this book to find all the questions within the book that deal with a specific topic. This allows you to focus specifically on areas that you particularly want to revise or, if you are mid-way through your course, it lets you practise answering exam-style questions for just those topics that you have studied.

Revision Advice

Work out a revision timetable for each week's work in advance – remember to cover all of your subjects and to leave time for homework and breaks. For example:

Day	6pm–6.45pm	7pm–8pm	8.15pm–9pm	9.15pm–10pm
Monday	Homework	Homework	English revision	Chemistry revision
Tuesday	Maths revision	Physics revision	Homework	Free
Wednesday	Geography revision	Modern Studies revision	English revision	French revision
Thursday	Homework	Maths revision	Chemistry revision	Free
Friday	Geography revision	French revision	Free	Free
Saturday	Free	Free	Free	Free
Sunday	Modern Studies revision	Maths revision	Modern Studies revision	Homework

Make sure that you have at least one evening free each week to relax, socialise and re-charge your batteries. It also gives your brain a chance to process the information that you have been feeding it all week.

Arrange your study time into sessions of 30 minutes or 1 hour, with a break between sessions e.g. 6pm–7pm, 7.15pm–7.45pm, 8pm–9pm. Try to start studying as early as possible in the evening when your brain is still alert and be aware that the longer you put off starting, the harder it will be to start!

Study a different subject in each session, except for the day before an exam.

Do something different during your breaks between study sessions – have a cup of tea, or listen to some music. Don't let your 15 minutes expanded into 20 or 25 minutes though!

Have your class notes and any textbooks available for your revision to hand as well as plenty of blank paper, a pen, etc. You may like to make keyword sheets like the geography example below:

Keyword	Meaning
Anticyclone	An area of high pressure
Secondary Industry	Industries that manufacture things
Erosion	The process of wearing down the landscape

Finally forget or ignore all or some of the advice in this section if you are happy with your present way of studying. Everyone revises differently, so find a way that works for you!

Transfer Your Knowledge

As well as using your class notes and textbooks to revise, these practice papers will also be a useful revision tool as they will help you to get used to answering exam-style questions. You may find as you work through the questions that they refer to a case study or an example that you haven't come across before. Don't worry! You should be able to transfer your knowledge of a topic or theme to a new example. The enhanced answer section at the back will demonstrate how to read and interpret the question to identify the topic being examined and how to apply your course knowledge in order to answer the question successfully.

Command Words

In the practice papers and in the exam itself, a number of command words will be used in the questions. These command words are used to show you how you should answer a question – some words indicate that you should write more than others. If you familiarise yourself with these command words, it will help you to structure your answers more effectively.

Command Word	Meaning/Explanation
Analyse	Explain why a writer has written in a certain way.
Argue	State the arguments for or against a case.
Challenge	Question what another person thinks or says.
Comment on	Explain and/or describe
Compare	Give the key features of two different items or ideas and discuss their similarities and/or their differences.
Convey	To put across, to communicate/to tell.
Critically evaluate	Judge the success of a particular text.
Define	Give the meaning of.
Describe	Write in detail about the features of a movement/ action/person/object.
Find evidence	Find quotes from the passage.
Express	Write/explain
Justify	Give reasons for your answer, stating why you have taken an action or reached a particular conclusion.
Suggest	Give an idea or suggestion.
Summarise	Condense into a shortened form.

In the Exam

Watch your time and pace yourself carefully. Work out roughly how much time you can spend on each answer and try to stick to this.

Be clear before the exam what the instructions are likely to be, for example how many questions you should answer in each section. The practice papers will help you to become familiar with the exam's instructions.

Read the question thoroughly before you begin to answer it – make sure you know exactly what the question is asking you to do. If the question is in sections e.g. 15a, 15b, 15c, etc, make sure that you can answer each section before you start writing.

Plan your answer by jotting down keywords, a mindmap or reminders of the important things to include in your answer. Cross them off as you deal with them and check them before you move on to the next question to make sure that you haven't forgotten anything.

Don't repeat yourself as you will not get any more marks for saying the same thing twice. This also applies to annotated diagrams, which will not get you any extra marks if the information is repeated in the written part of your answer.

Give proper explanations. A common error is to give descriptions rather than explanations. If you are asked to explain something, you should be giving reasons. Check your answer to an 'explain' question and make sure that you have used plenty of linking words and phrases such as 'because', 'this means that', 'therefore', 'so', 'so that', 'due to' and 'the reason is'.

Use the resources provided. Some questions will ask you to 'describe and explain' and provide an example or a case study for you to work from. Make sure that you take any relevant data from these resources.

Good luck!

Topic Index

Topic	General Reading Exam A ('Barn Owl Trust')	Credit Reading Exam A ('St Kilda')	General Reading Exam B ('The Lieutenant')	Credit Reading Exam B ('Star of the Sea')	General Reading Exam C ('Made in America')	Credit Reading Exam C ('The Man with No Name')
Understanding	1, 3, 4, 6, 7, 8, 10, 11, 12, 16	2, 3, 4, 5, 7(a/b), 8, 10, 11, 14	1, 3, 4, 5, 10, 11, 16	1(a), 2, 3, 4, 12, 15	1, 3, 4, 7	1(a), 2, 3, 16, 17
Finding Evidence	15	13	9, 19	16	7, 9(b), 12(c)	16, 5
Analysis	2, 5, 9, 13	1, 6, 7(c), 9, 12, 15, 16	2, 15	9, 16	2, 11	4, 13
Evaluation	18	17	22	13(a), 20	17, 18	8, 18, 19
Word Choice	2, 13	9, 15, 16	7	7, 11	6, 14	11, 12
Imagery		15	21	8	9	14
Sentence Structure	17	9	12	6	13	15

Exam A – General Paper

English   Standard Grade: General

Practice Papers
For SQA Exams

Answer all of the questions.

Read the following passage and then answer the questions. Remember to use your own words as
much as possible.

Scotland's leading educational publishers

The Barn Owl Trust

This passage is taken from the website of a charity called The Barn Owl Trust.

1. The Barn Owl Trust is a small charity working very hard to conserve one of the most beautiful birds on earth. Anyone who has ever watched a Barn Owl hunting at dusk has surely been touched by the experience but sadly these magical birds have become increasingly rare – and the reasons are all man-made. Lack of food due to intensive farming, the loss of roost and nest sites, road mortality, and a host of other factors are to blame.

2. We should remember, however, that the first reliable population estimate was not produced until 1999 and that evidence of the Barn Owl's historical decline in Britain is largely anecdotal. The often-quoted figure of a 70% decline between the 1930s and 1980s comes from the comparison of two unreliable population estimates. It's quite likely that Barn Owl decline started in the mid-1800s as a result of persecution by gamekeepers, egg collectors and the like. The fact is we shall never know to what extent these activities might have affected the Barn Owl population. Indeed they may have only caused the temporary reduction of local population levels.

3. Nevertheless, there is a strong consensus that Barn Owls must have been a lot more common before the mechanisation of farming. Before the late 1800s, when men and horses worked the land, farming was very much less intensive and there can be little doubt that wildlife in general was much more abundant. In particular, small mammals would have been much more common when there were more hedgerows, more marginal grazing land, and pasture was less intensively grazed. Stored cereal crops (in ricks or barns) became so infested with mice and rats that some enlightened farmers encouraged Barn Owls into their buildings via special access holes ('owl windows'). For a species that cannot hunt in rain and suffers high mortality in severe winters, imagine how indoor hunting might have helped survival.

4. In the late 1800s and early 1900s increasing human population levels and the proliferation of farm machines led to increases in the intensity of land management resulting in the loss of Barn Owl habitat. This accelerated during World War II with a drive for Britain to become more self-sufficient. The idea that British farmers had a duty to produce as much human food as possible (which became deeply ingrained during WWII) continued right up to the 1980s. Ask almost any elderly farmer and he'll probably remember seeing 'fluffy white owls' up on the barn wall when he was a lad in the 1930s. The changes in farming practices stimulated by the legacy of WWII, human population expansion, government policies, and consumer pressure for ever-cheaper food, are the main reason behind the Barn Owl's historical decline in Britain.

5. From the mid 1900s onwards, other factors started to work against the Barn Owl population: the proliferation of mouse and rat baits that kill predators as well as rodents; barns being converted into houses; the impact of the trunk road network (started in the 1950s) which now kills thousands of Barn Owls every year.

6   If the population is to expand, it is essential not only that traditional Barn Owl sites continue to be occupied but that the birds' breeding success is improved and that additional young birds disperse to occupy other sites. There are numerous factors that can cause the loss of occupied sites but fortunately most of these can be prevented by the implementation of sensible protection measures. Steps can also be taken to maximise nesting success and this has been a major part of the Barn Owl Trust's work since 1997 when we created a package of measures to be targeted at all known nest sites.

7   Simply contacting nest site owners and highlighting the owls' presence can go a long way towards securing their protection. Where the owner has plans to alter the site we advise on timing and incorporation of the owls' needs (for example making provision for owls in a barn conversion). We explain the owls' sensitivity to irregular disturbance and tolerance of regular activities. Food availability largely controls survival and nesting success so we identify patches of good habitat and explain their importance and advise on the creation of additional foraging areas. To minimise the chances of secondary poisoning we advise on alternative methods of rodent control.

8   As well as advisory work we carry out practical tasks. Very often the owls' nest place is not as safe as it could be – in particular, nests on ledges or in poorly designed nestboxes can result in young falling from the nest prematurely and dying of injury, neglect, or predation. We erect safer (deep) nestboxes. In case anything should happen to the main nest place we make alternative provision with a second nestbox, normally in another nearby building or tree. Steep-sided water troughs close to nests are a particular problem so we make special floats – one for each water tank within 200 metres of the nest to prevent owls from drowning.

9   Although compared to other charities the Barn Owl Trust is still very small, it has an impressive track record and an excellent reputation. It officially 'hatched' on the 30th July 1988 with the arrival of its registered charity number and a donation of £25 from one of its founding Trustees. That was all it had: a number, twenty-five pounds, and a few highly committed and very active volunteers!

10   In the early days effort was concentrated on habitat creation and boosting the number of wild Barn Owls by releasing additional birds from captivity. The Trust soon began highly detailed countywide surveys that highlighted the ongoing loss of occupied sites. This prompted a major research project looking at the effects of barn conversion on local Barn Owl populations, that in turn led to positive changes in Local Authority planning policies. Other projects have led to close working relationships with a wide range of conservation organisations.

11   Despite having a small team of professional staff and being consulted by government, the Barn Owl Trust is still a grass-roots voluntary organisation that prides itself on the sheer amount of practical work it does. Erecting nesting boxes, creating ideal habitats, providing quality care for injured owls, conducting innovative research and thought provoking educational work, organising specialist training for professionals – the Barn Owl Trust leads the field.

Look at Paragraph 1.

		Marks	

1. **Write down the one word** that best describes the work of the Barn Owl Trust.

   2 ■ 0

   [ ]

2. **Write down two words** that help to create a positive impression of Barn Owls.

   2 1 0

   [ ]   [ ]

3. **Write down one word** that tells us that there are many reasons why Barn Owls are becoming rare.

   2 ■ 0

   [ ]

Look at Paragraph 2.

4. **Write down a word** used later in the paragraph which means the same as 'anecdotal'.

   2 ■ 0

   [ ]

5. **Write down three words or expressions** which show that the writer is not certain about the facts.

   (i) _____

   (ii) _____

   (iii) _____

   2 1 0

Look at Paragraph 3.

6. Explain **in your own words** the most likely reason for the decline in Barn Owl numbers from the late 1880s onwards.

   _____

   _____

   2 1 0

	Marks	

7. (*a*) Why did some farmers encourage Barn Owls into their buildings?

_____

_____   **2 1 0**

(*b*) Why would this have been good for the Barn Owls?

_____

_____   **2 1 0**

Look at Paragraph 4.

8. (*a*) **Explain in your own words** why the loss of Barn Owl habitat increased during World War II.

_____

_____   **2 1 0**

(*b*) **In your own words**, give **one** other reason for the decline in the numbers of Barn Owls.

_____

_____   **2 ■ 0**

Look at Paragraph 5.

9. Explain the function **in this paragraph** of:

(*a*) the colon:

_____

_____   **2 1 0**

(*b*) the semicolons:

_____

_____   **2 1 0**

Look at Paragraph 6.

10. Tick the appropriate box to show whether the following statements are True, False, or you Can't Tell from the paragraph.

		True	False	Can't Tell			
(a)	There are three things that must happen if the Barn Owl population is to get bigger.				2	■	0
(b)	Using sensible protection measures will stop the loss of occupied sites.				2	■	0
(c)	The Barn Owl Trust has managed to maximise nesting success.				2	■	0

Look at Paragraph 7.

11. Which of the following is the best description of the **main topic** of the paragraph? Tick your choice of answer.

contacting site owners	
explaining owls' behaviour	
preventing the poisoning of owls	
giving advice about owls	

2 ■ 0

Look at Paragraph 8.

12. (a) **In your own words,** give one example of the 'practical tasks' carried out by the Trust.

_____

_____

2 1 0

(b) Explain the difference between 'advisory work' and 'practical tasks'.

_____

_____

2 1 0

Look at Paragraph 9.

13. **Write down two words or expressions** that create a good impression of the Barn Owl Trust.

(i) _____

(ii) _____

2 1 0

Marks

14. Why does the writer put inverted commas round the word 'hatched'?

_____

_____ | 2 | 1 | 0 |

Look at Paragraph 10.

15. What evidence is there that the Barn Owl Trust's work has been successful?

_____

_____ | 2 | 1 | 0 |

Look at Paragraph 11.

16. Write down an expression that means the opposite of 'grass roots volunteers'.

_____ | 2 | ■ | 0 |

17. Explain **the effect** of the following features of **sentence structure** in the last sentence of this paragraph.

(*a*) the list: _____

_____ | 2 | 1 | 0 |

(*b*) putting the main idea at the end: _____

_____ | 2 | 1 | 0 |

Think about the passage as a whole.

18. (i) What do you think is the **main purpose** of this piece of writing? Tick your choice.

to inform readers about Barn Owls	
to inform readers about the work of the Barn Owl Trust	

(ii) Justify your choice by referring to more than one part of the passage.

_____

_____

_____

_____ | 2 | 1 | 0 |

Exam A – Credit Paper

English   Standard Grade: Credit

Practice Papers
For SQA Exams

**Credit Level
Exam A
Reading**

Answer all of the questions.

Read the following passage and then answer the questions. Remember to use your own words as much as possible.

Scotland's leading educational publishers

St Kilda

In this article from The Scotsman *newspaper, Claire Black describes a visit to St Kilda.*

1   As I gaze across an endless choppy grey sea, smirr floats in the air, meets the spray from the boat, then falls back to the water. The Isle of Harris has long disappeared from the view behind us. Ahead there's only more water.

2   We've got another couple of hours to go until we reach our destination: St Kilda. The most remote part of the British Isles, an indelible part of Scotland's romantic history, the cluster of islands sits alone in the Atlantic, 41 miles west of Benbecula in the Outer Hebrides. It may welcome as many as 2000 day visitors each year, but only a handful of people get the opportunity to stay on the island. I'm one of them.

3   There are 11 of us bumping across the water, heading to the archipelago known as St Kilda, and most are trying to keep hold of our hastily eaten breakfast. I'm hitching a ride with a working party made up of experts from the National Trust for Scotland (NTS) and the Royal Commission on Ancient and Historical Monuments (RCAHMS), as well as five volunteers. As the archaeologists and surveyors continue their work mapping Hirta, the biggest island, the volunteers will carry out general maintenance work – painting roofs, clearing guttering, fixing a broken window and clearing drains. It's not glamorous, and they've paid for the privilege, but in exchange they'll get to spend two weeks on the island. Priceless.

4   St Kilda is one of only a few places in the world with Dual World Heritage status, recognising both its natural and cultural significance. Part of the island's appeal comes from the fact that it was evacuated of its remaining indigenous population in 1930. Struggling to survive, their numbers had dwindled and life on the island was becoming increasingly harsh. The place, and the lost lifestyle of the islanders – living in isolation, sharing their catch of seabirds and eggs which they clambered down the steep cliff faces to catch, ropes tied around their chests – intrigues us today just as it did the Victorian tourists who travelled to the island on steamers, to marvel at the St Kildans and buy their blown eggs or hand-spun wool as souvenirs.

5   I've got three days on the island to see at first hand the work that's being undertaken by the NTS and RCAHMS to survey Hirta, work that will be used to create the most detailed and accurate map of the islands ever completed. This will, in turn, help guide conservation work. A three-year project which began in 2007, it owes much to the groundbreaking work of archaeologist Dr Mary Harman, a St Kilda devotee. During the 1970s and 80s Harman created, largely on her own, the first detailed map of the islands. Scrambling down steep banks and vertiginous cliffs, she plotted the island's 1400 or so 'cleits', the small stone structures topped with turf that pepper Hirta, and can also be seen on the surrounding islands of Dun, Soay and Boreray.

6   These stone structures add to St Kilda's mystique (no one is quite sure what they were used for), as well as adding to its unique landscape. Harman is a hero to all the teams working on the island now and it's her field work which is now being combined with aerial photography and centimetre-accurate, satellite survey technology to plot all the known sites on Hirta as well as to locate new ones – ruins, the remains of structures, walls and even areas that have been farmed. Once the map is complete, as well as providing a unique and valuable record, it will help the NTS protect and maintain the remote landscape.

7   Suddenly, out of the greyness, St Kilda appears. Sheer cliffs rise from the sea. The air is speckled with seabirds – kittiwakes and gannets – swirling around the rock faces. The islands are home to more than half a million breeding seabirds – the largest colony in Europe – and the air is filled with their calls. As I'll discover, the legends and stories surrounding St Kilda far exceed what the islands themselves deliver, but at the same time they fail to capture its unique atmosphere.

8   The boat moored in the bay, I push a wheelbarrow filled with supplies up a wet, grassy verge, my legs still shaking from the journey. Soay sheep, the ancient fluffy brown breed unique to the island, glance disinterestedly as we straggle past. The 'village' on Hirta consists of one street. Of the cottages which line the street (built in 1860 after a visiting minister was appalled to see the islanders still shared their houses with cattle), five have been refurbished and provide accommodation for working parties. There's a communal kitchen and a small museum for day visitors to the island, as well as a store and two dorms. The others are roofless shells, but in the fireplace of each sits a slate painted with the name of the family who lived there before evacuation. It's a sight that's eerie and comforting at the same time.

9   Back outside, I sit on a small stone dyke to take in the view. It might look exactly as it did hundreds of years ago, apart from the Ministry of Defence base, now run by a defence technology company, down by the shoreline. Images of St Kilda are usually artfully cropped to remove signs of the base, its boxy buildings, the electricity generators and the helipad. They might not be part of the romantic view of the island but since the base (which is used as a radar tracking station for the missile range on Benbecula) was built in 1957, they are part of what the island is about. The Land Rover that zooms up the steep road twice a day as the receiver is checked is as much part of the island soundscape as the waves that lap on the stony beach.

10   As the sun breaks through the clouds, George Geddes, one of the National Trust's archaeologists guides me round the village area, showing me the traces of a head dyke which defined the area used for living and farming by the islanders and, of course, the cleits. Everywhere you look – up the steep slopes of the hills which loom over Village Bay – there are cleits of different sizes. Much of the mythology of St Kilda is built around these unique structures, which look something like igloos, but built with round-edged Dolomite stones and topped with turf. It's most likely that they were used as stores for keeping seabirds and eggs or for drying turf and peat, but it only adds to the romance that no one really knows. Most of the ones I pop my head into are full of sheep bones and fleece. Some of

them have additional cells joined to the main structure, some are large enough for ten people to stand inside, some so small that only a child could squeeze in. On the higher slopes, they look like smudges of stone or little bird boxes, gently sliding down the hill as time and the weather take their toll.

11 Clambering up the slopes behind the village, I stand at the top of vertiginous cliffs. The sky is piercing blue and kittiwakes glide and circle before landing in their cliff-face nests. Straight ahead, across a streak of the Atlantic that sparkles in the sunlight, stand Stac an Armin and Stac Lee, needlepoints of rock that rise high and proud, beside the island of Boreray, seven miles from Hirta. On a day like this the rocky outcrops look benign, but for the St Kildans who travelled in small rowing boats to collect seabirds and their eggs, they could be treacherous. It wasn't unknown for hunting parties to be stranded by bad weather, forced to take shelter in the cleits until they could return safely.

12 As I trample back down the hill, Village Bay looks like a mouth gulping in the ocean. As the light fades, I'm standing on the end of a stone pier and soon the darkness will be inky black. Shiny waves slap the spray-covered stone and the wind whips around.

Look at Paragraphs 1 to 3.

		Marks	

1. Give **three** ways in which the writer emphasises a sense of isolation in Paragraphs 1 and 2.

    (i) _____

    (ii) _____

    (iii) _____   2 1 0

2. '… the archipelago known as St Kilda …' (Paragraph 3)

    Write down an expression used earlier in the passage that helps you understand what an 'archipelago' is.

    _____   2 ■ 0

3. In what ways is the visit 'not glamorous' for the volunteers?

    _____

    _____   2 1 0

Look at Paragraph 4.

4. 'recognising both its natural and cultural significance'

    In your own words explain what is meant by

    (i) '**natural** significance': _____

    _____   2 ■ 0

    (ii) '**cultural** significance': _____

    _____   2 ■ 0

5. Explain **in your own words** why the islanders were evacuated from the island in 1930.

    _____

    _____   2 1 0

| | | Marks | |

6. What is the function of the information given between the dashes in this paragraph?

_____

_____ | 2 | 1 | 0 |

Look at Paragraphs 5 and 6.

7. (*a*) What is the main purpose of the work currently being undertaken by the NTS and the RCAHMS?

_____ | 2 | ■ | 0 |

(*b*) Explain **in your own words** the importance of Dr Mary Harman to this work.

_____ | 2 | 1 | 0 |

(*c*) By **quoting words or expressions**, show how the writer contrasts the way Dr Harman worked and the way the work is carried out now.

Dr Harman	now

| 2 | ■ | 0 |

8. In what way do cleits 'add to St Kilda's mystique'?

_____

_____ | 2 | 1 | 0 |

Look at Paragraph 7.

9. Show how the writer uses **word choice** and **sentence structure** to make this paragraph dramatic.

Word choice: _____

_____ | 2 | 1 | 0 |

Sentence structure: _____

_____ | 2 | 1 | 0 |

	Marks	

10. In your own words explain two ways in which the 'legends and stories surrounding St Kilda' are unsatisfactory as far as the writer is concerned.

(i) _____

_____   **2 1 0**

(ii) _____

_____   **2 1 0**

Look at Paragraph 8.

11. 'glance disinterestedly as we straggle past'

Tick the box beside the best definition of 'disinterestedly'.

in a neutral way	
in a careless way	
in a bored way	
in a bemused way	

2 ■ 0

12. Why has the writer put inverted commas around the word 'village'?

_____

_____   **2 ■ 0**

13. 'It's a sight that's eerie and comforting at the same time'.

Explain why the writer feels each of these emotions when she sees the names on the slates.

(i) eerie:_____

_____   **2 1 0**

(ii) comforting:_____

_____   **2 1 0**

Look at Paragraph 9.

14. (*a*) Explain **in your own words** why 'images of St Kilda are usually cropped to remove signs of the base'.

_____

_____

2 | 1 | 0

(*b*) Explain **in your own words** why the writer thinks this is not appropriate.

_____

_____

2 | 1 | 0

Look at Paragraph 10.

15. By referring to details or individual words in this paragraph, explain **two** ways in which the writer makes clear how mysterious cleits are.

(i) _____

_____

2 | 1 | 0

(ii) _____

_____

2 | 1 | 0

Look at Paragraphs 11 and 12.

16. Write down **three** words or expressions that help to create a romantic picture of the scene.

(i) _____

(ii) _____

(iii) _____

2 | 1 | 0

17. Referring to **at least one** detail in Paragraph 12, say whether you think the paragraph is an effective way to end **the passage as a whole**.

_____

_____

_____

2 | 1 | 0

English   Standard Grade: General

Answer all of the questions.

Read the following passage and then answer the questions. Remember to use your own words as much as possible.

The Lieutenant

In the opening chapter of Kate Grenville's novel 'The Lieutenant', the author describes Daniel Rooke's early schooldays.

1   Daniel Rooke was quiet, moody, a man of few words. He had no memories other than of being an outsider.

2   At the dame school* in Portsmouth they thought him stupid. His first day there was by coincidence his fifth birthday, the third of March 1767. He took his place behind the desk with his mother's breakfast oatmeal cosy in his stomach and his new jacket on, happy to be joining the world beyond his home. Mrs Bartholomew showed him a badly executed engraving with the word 'cat' underneath. His mother had taught him his letters and he had been reading for a year. He could not work out what Mrs Bartholomew wanted. He sat at his desk, mouth open.

3   That was the first time he was paddled* with Mrs Bartholomew's old hairbrush for failing to respond to a question so simple he had not thought to answer it.

4   He could not become interested in the multiplication tables. While the others chanted through them, impatient for the morning break, he was looking under the desk at the notebook in which he was collecting his special numbers, the ones that could not be divided by any number but themselves and one. Like him, they were solitaries*.

5   When Mrs Bartholomew pounced on him one day and seized the notebook, he was afraid she would throw it in the fire and smack him with the hairbrush again. She looked at it for a long time and put it away in her pinny* pocket.

6   He wanted to ask for it back. Not for the numbers, they were in his head, but for the notebook, too precious to lose.

7   Then Dr Adair from the Academy came to the house in Church Street. Rooke could not guess who Dr Adair was, or what he was doing in their parlour*. He only knew that he had been washed and combed for a visitor, that his infant sisters had been sent next door to the neighbour woman, and that his mother and father were sitting on the uncomfortable chairs in the corner with rigid faces.

8   Dr Adair leaned forward. Did Master Rooke know of numbers that could be divided by nothing but themselves and one? Rooke forgot to be in awe. He ran up to his attic room and came back with the grid he had drawn, ten by ten, the first hundred numbers with these special ones done in red ink: two, three, five and on to ninety-seven. He pointed, there was a kind of pattern, do you see, here and here? But one hundred numbers was not enough, he needed a bigger sheet of paper so he could make a square twenty or even thirty a side, and then he could find the true pattern, and perhaps Dr Adair might be able to provide him with such a sheet?

9   His father by now had the rictus* of a smile that meant his son was exposing his oddness to a stranger, and his mother was looking down into her lap. Rooke folded the grid and hid it under his hand on the table.

10   But Dr Adair lifted his fingers from the grubby paper. 'May I borrow this?' he asked. 'I would like, if I may, to show it to a gentleman of my acquaintance who will be interested that it was created by a boy of seven.'

11   After Dr Adair went, the neighbour woman brought his sisters back. She inspected Rooke and said loudly, as if he were deaf, or a dog, 'Yes, he looks clever, don't he?' Rooke felt the hairs on his head standing up with the heat of his blush. Whether it was because he was stupid or clever, it added up to the same thing: the misery of being out of step with the world.

12   When he turned eight Dr Adair offered the bursary*. It was just words: *a place at the Portsmouth Naval Academy*. The boy thought it could not be too different from the life he knew, went along blithely and hardly waved goodbye to his father at the gate. The first night there he lay rigid in the dark, too shocked to cry.

13   The other boys established that his father was a clerk who went every day to the squat stone building near the docks where the Office of Ordnance ran its affairs. In the world of Church Street, Benjamin Rooke was a man of education and standing, a father to be proud of. At the Portsmouth Naval Academy a mile away, he was an embarrassment. *A clerk! Oh dearie me*! A boy took everything out of his trunk, the shirts and underthings his mother and grandmother had so carefully made, and hurled them through the window into the muddy yard three flights below. A man in a billowing black gown caught Rooke painfully by the ear and hit him with a cane when he tried to say that he had not done it. A big boy sat him up on a high wall out behind the kitchens and poked him with a stick until he was forced to jump down.

14   His ankle still hurt from the fall, but that was not the pain at his heart.

15   His attic in Church Street wrapped its corners and angles around him, the shape of his own odd self. At the Academy, the cold space of the bleak dormitory sucked out his spirit and left a shell behind.

16   Walking from the Academy back to Church Street every Saturday evening to spend Sunday at home was a journey between one world and another that wrenched him out of shape each time. His mother and father were so proud, so warm with pleasure that their clever son had been singled out, that he could not tell them how he felt. His grandmother might have understood, but he could not find the words to tell even her how he had lost himself.

17 When it came time for him to walk back, Anne held his hand with both hers, pulling at him with all her child's weight and crying for him to stay. She was not yet five, but somehow knew that he longed to remain anchored in the hallway. His father peeled her fingers away one by one and shooed him out the door, waving and smiling, so that Rooke had to wave too and put a grin on his face. All the way up the street he could hear Anne wailing, and his nan trying to comfort her.

dame school	a type of private primary school run by women
paddled	to be spanked or beaten with a small bat
solitaries	used here to mean prime numbers, i.e. numbers that can only be divided by themselves and one
pinny	shortened form of 'pinafore', which is an apron or overall for women
parlour	a family sitting room or living room
rictus	fixed, open mouth
bursary	a sum of money given to a pupil in financial need to pay for his or her education

Read paragraph 1 again

		Marks	

1. What did Daniel remember about his childhood?

_____

_____

| 2 | 1 | 0 |

2. Why was 3rd of March 1767 an important date for Daniel?

_____

_____

| 2 | 1 | 0 |

3. In your own words, explain why the teachers at the dame school thought Daniel was 'stupid' (paragraph 2) on his first day at the school.

_____

_____

| 2 | 1 | 0 |

4. Explain in your own words how Mrs Bartholemew reacted to Daniel's silence when she showed him the engraving.

_____

_____

| 2 | ■ | 0 |

5. Explain in your own words why Daniel 'could not become interested in the multiplication tables'? (paragraph 4)

_____

_____

| 2 | 1 | 0 |

6. 'Like him, they were solitaries'. (paragraph 4) What does this expression tell you about Daniel? Refer to the glossary if you need to.

_____

_____

| 2 | 1 | 0 |

7. Explain <u>how</u> Mrs Bartholemew took Daniel's notebook. Quote from paragraph 5 to support your answer.

_____

_____

| 2 | 1 | 0 |

8. Why do you think Mrs Bartholemew (a) 'looked at it for a long time and (b) put it away in her pinny pocket'? (paragraph 5)

(*a*) _____

(*b*) _____

| 2 | 1 | 0 |

	Marks	

9. Did Daniel <u>need</u> or <u>want</u> the book back? Explain your choice, quoting from the passage to support your answer.

_____

_____

2 1 0

10. In what way did the family make an effort to impress Dr Adair? Answer in your own words.

_____

_____

2 1 0

11. How does the writer show that Daniel is not 'in awe' (paragraph 8) of Dr Adair?

_____

_____

2 1 0

12. 'But one hundred numbers … such a sheet.' (paragraph 8) What is unusual about this sentence structure and why has it been used?

_____

_____

2 1 0

13. How did his father feel when Daniel was showing the grid to Dr Adair?

_____

_____

2 ■ 0

14. Why does Dr Adair wish to show Daniel's grid to a friend of his?

_____

_____

2 1 0

Read paragraphs 10 and 11 again.

15. What is the difference between the language Dr Adair uses to speak to Rooke in paragraph 10 and the language the neighbour woman uses to speak to Rooke in paragraph 11?

_____

_____

2 1 0

16. Read paragraph 12 beginning 'When he turned eight.' Explain in your own words how Daniel first felt about attending Portsmouth Naval Academy.

_____

_____

2 1 0

	Marks	

17. *'A clerk! Oh dearie me!'* (Paragraph 13) Suggest who might have spoken these words and why.

_____

_____ | 2 | 1 | 0 |

18. On Daniel's first night at the Academy, he is 'too shocked to cry'. (paragraph 12) Give two examples of things that happened at the Academy on his first day that might have made him shocked.

    (*a*) _____

    (*b*) _____ | 2 | 1 | 0 |

19. Read paragraph 15 again. Explain in your own words how Daniel felt
    (*a*) at his home in the attic in Church Street

    _____ | 2 | 1 | 0 |

    (*b*) in the dormitory at the Academy

    _____ | 2 | 1 | 0 |

20. Write down an expression in Paragraph 16 which emphasises the contrast between Daniel's home and school.

    _____

    _____ | 2 | ■ | 0 |

21. Why did Daniel feel he could not explain his true feelings to his parents?

    _____

    _____ | 2 | 1 | 0 |

22. Daniel's sister Anne knew that Daniel wanted to 'remain anchored in the hallway'. (paragraph 17)
    (*a*) What technique has the writer used here?

    _____ | 2 | ■ | 0 |

    (*b*) What does this tell you about how Daniel feels about his home and family?

    _____ | 2 | ■ | 0 |

Think about the passage as a whole.

23. This extract comes from the opening of the novel 'The Lieutenant', which tells the story of Daniel's life and search for a sense of 'belonging'. Do you think that this opening is effective in introducing Daniel's life? Answer fully, quoting from the passage to support your answer.

    _____

    _____

    _____

    _____ | 2 | 1 | 0 |

Exam B – Credit Paper

English   Standard Grade: Credit

Answer all of the questions.

Read the following passage and then answer the questions. Remember to use your own words as much as possible.

Star of the Sea

In this passage from 'Star of the Sea' by Joseph O'Connor, Grantley Dixon is sailing to America aboard the 'Star of the Sea' in 1847. Dixon wants to become a famous writer but a publisher, Newby, has recently rejected his collection of short stories and has given him a novel written by a minister from the north of England to read.

1   Dixon had wasted all of yesterday on the northern vicar's dreary novel. The wind was high and the sea choppy and Laura had said she wanted time to be alone. She was acting very strangely since they had boarded the ship, making excuses to avoid speaking to him or being in his company. Perhaps she was right to be alone.

2   The morning had begun with reasonable calm: a glitter of cold sunlight on a greygreen of water. He had sat outside the Breakfast Room intending to kill a few hours in reading. A single drop of rain had smacked the title page as he opened the cover. Within five minutes the sky had darkened to the colour of lead.

3   'Put up the lifelines. And get the passengers below.'

4   Sailors were already running. Lightening flickered in the bulbous thickness of the clouds; it lit them up in a crackling explosion. A powerful gust buffeted the mainmast, sending reverberations down to the maindeck and shattering crockery and glasses in the Breakfast Room behind him. The ship gave a nauseating undulation; a lurch; a sway. The shutters were being wound down, the canopy chained up. A steward hurrying past with a stack of chairs had shouted at him to get below but Grantley Dixon had not moved.

5   The music of the ship was howling around him. The low whistlings; the tortured rumbles; the wheezy sputters of breeze flowing through it. The clatter of loose wainscoting. The clank of chains. The groaning of boards. The blare of wind. Never before had he felt rain quite like it. It seemed to spew from the clouds, not merely to fall. He watched the wave rise up from a quarter of a mile away. Rolling. Foaming. Rushing. Surging. Beginning to thicken and swell in strength. Now it was a battlement of ink-black water, almost crumpling under its own weight; but still rising, and now roaring. It smashed into the side of the buckling *Star*, like a punch thrown by an invisible god. He was aware of being flung backwards into the edge of a bench, the dull crack of metal against the base of his spine. The ship creaked violently and pitched into a tilt, downing slowly, almost on to beam ends. A clamour of terrified screams rose up from steerage. A hail of cups and splintering plates. A man's bellow: 'Knockdown! Knockdown!' One of the starboard lifeboats snapped from its bow-chain and swung loose like a mace, shattering through the wall of the wheelhouse.

6   The boom of the billows striking the prow a second time. A blind of salt lashed him; drenched him through. Waves churning over his body. The slip of his body down the boards towards the water. A shredding *skreek* of metal on metal. The grind of the engine ripped from the ocean. The ship began to right itself.

Snappings of wood filled the air like gunshots. The wail of the klaxon being sounded for clear-all-decks. The man with the club-foot was helping a sailor to grab a woman who was being swept on her back towards the broken rail. She was screaming in terror; grasping; clutching. Somehow they seized her and dragged her below. Hand by hand, gripping the slimy life-rope like a mountaineer, Dixon made it back to the First-Class deckhouse.

7   Two stewards were in the passageway distributing canisters of soup. Passengers were to retire to their quarters immediately. There was no need for concern. The storm would pass. It was entirely to be expected. A matter of the season. The ship could not capsize; it never had in eighty years. The lifebelts were merely a matter of precaution. But the Captain had ordered everyone to remain below. Laura looking pleadingly at him from the end of the corridor, her terrified sons bawling into her skirts. The three of them being grabbed by an angry-faced Merridith and dragged into her cabin like sacks.

8   'Inside, sir. Inside! Don't come out until you're called.'

9   He had found dry clothes and eaten all his soup. After an hour, the storm had levelled down a little. The Chief Steward had knocked on his door with a message from the Captain. All passengers were strictly confined for the rest of the day. No exceptions whatsoever were permitted. The hatches were about to be battened down.

10 He had tried to settle, to read again, as the pitch of the ocean flung breakers against the porthole and the shrill of the wind surged up and down the roof. But the novel had not done much to improve his spirits.

11 Yes, it had passion or passion of a sort: the usual tiresome show-off gushiness. Here and there it managed to stagger into weary life, only to be crushed by the weight of the prose style. Like most first novels, like Dixon's own, it was an attempt at a story of physical love. But it was wildly over-ambitious, peopled by puppets. The way it so flagrantly strained for its effects let it down. Reading it was like trudging through a peatbog in Connemara. A few startling flowers among a wilderness of sog.

12 *I have no pity! I have no pity! The more the worms writhe, the more I yearn to crush out their entrails!*

13 Sweet Christ.

14 How could yet more of this sludge be pumped into the world when his own carefully constructed pieces had been rejected? Newby had been correct to think it would fail. No critic in his right mind would give this eructation* a good notice. It was confused, improbable, disjointed, vague. Precisely the quality for which he had striven in his own writing - a respect for the actual meanings of words – was entirely and woefully missing from this.

15 And yet, he knew, Laura would love it. She who had damned with the faintest of praise would adore this florid* and juvenile monstrosity; this compendium of adjectives and schoolboy neuroses. She would think it 'aesthetic', high-minded, moving. It was laughable, sometimes, the way she prattled on. If he didn't love her so much, he often thought he would detest her.

eructation   belch or burp
florid   showy, excessively detailed

1. (*a*) How did Dixon feel about the novel he is reading?

_____

_____ | 2 | 1 | 0 |

(*b*) Quote a phrase from paragraph 2 which continues this idea.

[   ]

2 | ■ | 0

2. **In your own words**, suggest why Laura might have wanted time to be alone the previous day.

_____

_____ | 2 | 1 | 0 |

3. Read paragraph 2 again. Why might the storm have come as a surprise to the passengers and crew of the ship?

_____

_____ | 2 | 1 | 0 |

4. Suggest who gave the instruction 'Put up the lifelines. And get the passengers below.' (paragraph 3) Give a reason for your answer.

_____

_____ | 2 | 1 | 0 |

5. Read again paragraph 4 starting 'Sailors were already running.'
Tick the best definition of 'reverberations'. | 2 | ■ | 0 |

echoes ☐
vibrations ☐
memories ☐
reflections ☐

6. 'The ship gave a nauseating undulation; a lurch; a sway.' (paragraph 4)

Comment on the sentence structure used here.

_____

_____ | 2 | 1 | 0 |

		Marks	

7. Comment on the effectiveness of the writer's word choice in the phrase 'The music of the ship'(paragraph 5), referring to the sentences which follow this phrase in your answer.

_____

_____

_____   **2 1 0**

8. 'like a punch thrown by an invisible god' (paragraph 5)

Explain in your own words whether you find this image effective.

_____

_____   **2 1 0**

9. 'He was aware of being flung…' to 'wheelhouse'. (paragraph 5) Identify the mood or atmosphere the writer creates in these lines and what techniques he uses to create this.

_____

_____   **2 1 0**

10. Write down an expression in paragraph 5 which means   **2 1 0**

(*a*) loud noise made by a number of people

_____

(*b*) loud noise made by an individual

_____

11. Dixon hears the '*skreek* of metal on metal'. (paragraph 6) Comment fully on the writer's word choice here.

_____

_____   **2 1 0**

12. Why might it have been difficult for the man and the sailor to rescue the woman who was being swept towards the broken rail?

_____

_____   **2 1 0**

				Marks	

13. (*a*) How convincing do you find the instructions the two stewards give the passengers as they distribute the canisters of soup?

_____

_____

2 1 0

(*b*) Who gives an instruction which contradicts what the stewards have said and, in your own words, how does it contradict the stewards?

_____

_____

2 1 0

14. 'Inside, sir. Inside! Don't come out until you're called.' (paragraph 8) What is the emotion of the speaker here? Discuss how the writer's language conveys this feeling.

_____

_____

2 1 0

15. 'But the novel had not done much to improve his spirits.'

Quote THREE criticisms Dixon makes about the minister's novel in the paragraph following this sentence.

1 _____

2 _____

3 _____

2 1 0

16. *'I have no pity! I have no pity! The more the worms writhe, the more I yearn to crush out their entrails!'* (paragraph 12)

Comment fully on the language of this short extract from the minister's novel. You might discuss word choice, punctuation, sentence structure or any other aspect of the language used.

_____

_____

2 1 0

		Marks		

17. 'How could yet more of this sludge be pumped into the world when his own carefully constructed pieces had been rejected?' (paragraph 14)

    (a) Explain fully in your own words why Dixon is annoyed that his own novel has been rejected and that the minister's might be accepted for publication?

_____

_____   2   1   0

    (b) Which technique is used to convey this annoyance to the reader?

_____   2   ■   0

18. 'And yet, he knew, Laura would love it.' (paragraph 15). Explain fully the function of the word 'yet' in this sentence.

_____

_____   2   1   0

19. 'If he didn't love her so much, he often thought he would detest her,'

In your own words, what reasons does Grantley give for 'detesting' Laura?

_____

_____   2   1   0

20. How successful is the writer in conveying the unpleasant and harsh conditions on board the Star of the Sea? Refer to ideas in the passage to support your answer.

_____

_____

_____   2   1   0

Think about the passage as a whole.

21. Do you feel sympathy or lack of sympathy for Grantley Dixon and Laura?

Justify your choice by close reference to the passage.

    (a) Grantley Dixon

_____

_____   2   1   0

    (b) Laura

_____

_____   2   1   0

English Standard Grade: General

Practice Papers
For SQA Exams

General Level
Exam C
Reading

Answer all of the questions.

Read the following passage and then answer the questions. Remember to use your own words as much as possible.

Made in America

In this extract from 'Made in America', the writer Bill Bryson describes how McDonald's has grown into a multi-million pound business.

1   As late as 1950, pork was still the most widely eaten meat in America, and by a considerable margin, but over the next two decades the situation was reversed. By 1970 Americans were eating twice as much beef as pork, nearly a hundred pounds of it a year, and half of that in the form of hamburgers. One company more than any other was responsible for this massive change in dietary habits: McDonald's.

2   The story as conveyed by the company is well known. A salesman of Multimixers named Ray Kroc became curious as to why a small hamburger stand on the edge of the desert in San Bernardino, California, would need eight Multimixers – enough to make forty milk-shakes at a time, more than any other restaurant in American could possibly want to make – and decided to fly out and have a look. The restaurant he found, run by the brothers Maurice and Richard McDonald, was small, only 600 square feet, but the burgers were tasty, the fries crisp, the shakes unusually thick, and it was unquestionably popular with the locals. Kroc at this time was fifty-two years old, an age when most men would be thinking of slowing down, but he saw an opportunity here. He bought the McDonald's name and began building an empire. The implication has always been that the original McDonald's was an obscure, rinky-dink operation in the middle of nowhere, and that it was only the towering genius of Ray Kroc that made it into the streamlined, efficient, golden-arched institution that we know and love today. It wasn't entirely like that.

3   By 1954, when Kroc came along, the McDonald brothers were already legendary, at least in the trade. *American Restaurant* magazine had done a cover story on them in 1952, and they were constantly being visited by people who wanted to see how they generated so much turnover from so little space. With sales of over $350,000 a year (all of it going through one busy cash register) and profits above $100,000, McDonald's was one of the most successful restaurants in America. In his autobiography, Kroc makes it sound as if the McDonald brothers had never thought of franchising until he came along. In fact, by the time he visited them they had a dozen franchised operations going.

4   Almost everything later associated with the McDonald's chain was invented or perfected by the brothers, from the method of making French fries to the practice of trumpeting the number of hamburgers sold. As early as 1950, they had a sign outside announcing 'Over 1 Million Sold'. They even came up with the design of a sloping roof, red and white tiled walls and integral golden arches – not for the San Bernardino outlet but for their first franchise operation, which opened in Phoenix in 1952, two years before Kroc came along.

5   The McDonald's were, in short, the true heroes of the fast-food revolution, and by any measure they were remarkable men. They had moved to California from New Hampshire (or possibly Vermont; sources conflict) during the depression years, and opened their first drive-in restaurant in 1937 near Pasadena. It didn't

sell hamburgers. Then in 1940 they opened a new establishment at Fourteenth and E Streets, at the end of Route 66, in San Bernardino in a snug octagonal structure. It was a conventional hamburger stand, and it did reasonably well.

6   In 1948, however, the brothers were seized with a strange vision. They closed the business for three months, fired the twenty carhops, got rid of all the china and silverware, and reopened with a new, entirely novel idea: that the customer would have to come to a window to collect the food rather than have it brought to the car. They cut the menu to just seven items – hamburgers, cheeseburgers, pie, crisps, coffee, milk and pop. Customers no longer specified what they wanted on their hamburgers but received them with ketchup, mustard, onions and pickle. The hamburgers were made smaller – just ten to a pound – but the price was halved to fifteen cents each.

7   The change was a flop. Business fell by 80 per cent. The teenagers on whom they had relied went elsewhere. Gradually, however, a new type of clientele developed, the family, particularly after they added French fries and milk shakes to the menu, and even more particularly when customers realised that the food was great and that you could feed a whole family for a few dollars. Before long McDonald's had almost more business than it could handle.

8   As volume grew, the brothers constantly refined the process to make the production of food more streamlined and efficient. With a local machine-shop owner named Ed Toman they invented almost everything connected with the production of fast food, from dispensers that pump out a precise dollop of ketchup or mustard to the Lazy Susans on which twenty-four hamburger buns can be speedily dressed. They introduced the idea of specialization – one person who did nothing but cook hamburgers, another who make shakes, another to dress the buns, and so on – and developed the now universal practice of having the food prepared and waiting so that customers could place an order and immediately collect it.

franchising   selling a licence to an individual who can then use a company's name and sell its products.

		Marks	

1. (a) What changed in the American diet between 1950 and 1970?

   _____

   _____ | 2 | 1 | 0 |

   (b) Which company was responsible for this change? Quote to support your answer.

   _____

   _____ | 2 | 1 | 0 |

2. 'as conveyed by the company'. What does this expression tell you about the writer's attitude towards McDonald's?

   _____

   _____ | 2 | 1 | 0 |

3. Why was Ray Kroc curious about the 'small hamburger stand' in California?

   _____

   _____ | 2 | ■ | 0 |

4. What made the restaurant popular, according to Ray Kroc?

   _____

   _____ | 2 | 1 | 0 |

5. Why does the writer mention Ray Kroc's age? Answer in your own words.

   _____

   _____ | 2 | 1 | 0 |

6. (a) The writer suggests that McDonald's was originally a 'rinky-dink operation'. (paragraph 2) Explain **in your own words** what this means.

   _____

   _____ | 2 | ■ | 0 |

   (b) Give an example of a word later in the paragraph which <u>contrasts</u> with this idea.

   [   ] | 2 | ■ | 0 |

7. By 1954, the McDonald brothers were already famous. Give **two** pieces of evidence from the text to support this claim.

   (a) _____

   (b) _____ | 2 | 1 | 0 |

		Marks

8. Why do you think Ray Kroc might want people to think that he was the first person to think of buying a McDonald's franchise?

_____

_____   2 | 1 | 0

9. 'trumpeting the number of hamburgers sold' (paragraph 4).

(*a*) What **technique** does the writer use here and what does it tell you about how McDonald's communicated its huge sales numbers?

_____

_____   2 | 1 | 0

(*b*) Give an example of how McDonald's were 'trumpeting' the numbers of hamburgers sold.

_____

_____   2 | 1 | 0

10. Read paragraph 3 again. What happened in both 1952 and 1954?

1952 _____

1954 _____   2 | 1 | 0

11. Write down **two** expressions the writer uses in **paragraph 5** to show that he admires the McDonald brothers.

(*a*) _____

(*b*) _____   2 | 1 | 0

12. In 1948, the McDonald brothers had a 'strange vision'. (paragraph 6)

(*a*) What was their 'strange vision'?

_____

_____   2 | 1 | 0

(*b*) Name two changes the brothers made to the menu in 1948.

(i) _____

(ii) _____   2 | 1 | 0

(c) Write down an expression from paragraph 5 which means the same as 'original'.

_____   2 | ■ | 0

13. Why are dashes used around the expration '– just ten to the pound –'.(paragraph 6)

_____

_____   2 | 1 | 0

14. 'The change was a flop'. (paragraph 7) Comment on the word choice in this sentence.

_____

_____

Marks
2 1 0

15. To whom did the new McDonalds restaurants appeal and why?

_____

_____

2 1 0

16. As the business grew, what did the brothers do to make food production more efficient?

_____

_____

2 1 0

Think about the passage as a whole.

17. (*a*) Do you think customers enjoyed eating at McDonald's? Answer fully, referring to the passage to support your answer.

_____

_____

2 1 0

(*b*) Do you think employees enjoyed working at McDonald's? Answer fully, referring to the passage to support your answer.

_____

_____

2 1 0

18. In your opinion, what is the purpose of this extract? Tick the purpose you think best fits the extract. Give a reason for your answer.

(*a*) To advertise McDonald's ☐

(*b*) To criticize how McDonald's is run ☐

(*c*) To give the true story about McDonald's ☐

_____

_____

2 1 0

19. This extract comes from a chapter entitled 'Welcome to the Space Age: The 1950s and Beyond'. Do you find this title appropriate? Give a reason for your answer

_____

_____

2 1 0

Exam C – Credit Paper

English   Standard Grade: Credit

Practice Papers
For SQA Exams

**Credit Level
Exam C
Reading**

Answer all of the questions.

Read the following passage and then answer the questions. Remember to use your own words as much as possible.

The Man With No Name

John Pilger, in a newspaper article from 1991, writes about the problem of homelessness in London, which he blames on the Government.

1   When it was raining hard the other day, a familiar silhouette appeared at my front door. I knew it was him, because, having rung the bell, he retreated to the gate: a defensive habit gained on the streets. 'It's the man', said my young daughter, 'with no name.'

2   He had on his usual tie and tweed jacket and was leaning against the hedge, though he said he hadn't had a drink. 'Just passing through,' he said as usual, and money passed between us with the customary clumsy handshake. 'I'd better give that a trim,' he said, as he always did, pointing at the hedge, and again I thanked him and said no; he was too unsteady for that. Collar up, he turned back into the rain.

3   I have known him for about three years. He comes to my door at least every week, and I see him out on the common in all weathers, asleep or reading or looking at traffic. I see him nodding as if in silent discussion with himself on a weighty matter; or waving and smiling at a procession of women with small children in buggies. Understandably, women hurry away from him; others look through him.

4   He has no home, although he once told me he lived 'just around the corner'. That turned out to be a hostel. From what I can gather, he sleeps rough most of the time, often on a bench in front of a small powerboats clubhouse, or in a clump of large trees where sick and alcoholic men go and where there was a murder some years back. In winter, he has newspapers tucked inside his jacket. Perhaps he is fifty, or more; it's difficult to tell.

5   He vanishes from time to time, as the homeless tend to do; and when I last asked him about this, he said he went to 'visit my sister'. I very much doubted this; I know he goes to one of several seaside towns for a few weeks at a time. There he scans the local newspaper small ads for 'unemployed guests wanted'. These are inserted by the owners of bed-and-breakfast hotels and hostels, where homeless people are sent by local authorities and by the Department of Health and Social Security.

6   I can imagine a little of what it must be like for him. As a reporter I once ended up in one of these 'hotels'. When I couldn't produce the Social Security form that would allow the owner to collect every penny of his 'guest's' state benefit, I was thrown out.

7　My friend is one of 80,000 people who are officially homeless in London. This is the equivalent of the population of Stevenage, in Hertfordshire; the true figure is greater, of course. The national figure for homeless households is 169,000, ten times higher than a decade ago. The homeless are now a nation within a nation, whose suffering makes a good television story at Christmas or when there is snow and ice.

8　I have never been made homeless. To have nowhere to go, perhaps for the rest of my life, to face every day the uncertainty of night and fear of the elements, is almost unimaginable.

9　My friend is typical in that he bears the familiar scars of homelessness: such as a furtiveness that gives the impression of a person being followed; a sporadic, shallow joviality that fails to mask his anxiety; and a deferential way that does not necessarily reflect his true self. The latter, because it is out of character, is occasionally overtaken by melodramatic declarations of independence. When he told me he had to go to hospital one day for a stomach operation and I offered to take him, he said, 'No! I can walk! Of course I can!' And he did.

10　I didn't know who or what he was until recently. It seemed an intrusion to ask. My place in his life was simply as a source of a few quid from time to time. Then one day he was telling me about a television programme about Asia he had seen, and it was clear he had been there in the Army. And that led to a statement of pride about what he had done with his life on leaving the Army. He had worked in a garage, training apprentice mechanics, until this was thwarted by a string of personal tragedies: a divorce and finally his 'redundancy': that wonderful expression of the Enterprise Society. He was then too old to start again; and he was taking to drink.

11　He has turned up with cuts and bruises, and blood caked on his cheek. Once, when I said I would go and call a doctor, I returned to the door to find him gone. On the common and in the streets, he is prey to thugs and to the police. He has little of the protection the rest of us assume as a right, provided by a civilised society.

12　Recently it was National Housing Week. The junior housing minister, Tim Yeo, said the government's 'rough sleepers initiative', which was launched during the freezing conditions of last winter, had halved the numbers of homeless sleeping out in London.

13　Anyone driving through London's West End knows this to be untrue. The homeless in the capital have become a tourist curiosity. Europeans are incredulous at having to step over so many human bundles on the pavement, in the Underground, on the steps of galleries and museums. Eavesdrop on a French tour guide describing the sights in the shopfronts of the Strand. 'They were hosed away,' she says, 'but they have come back.'

1. (a) Why does 'the man with no name' visit the writer?

_____ **2 ■ 0**

(b) The 'man with no name' visits the writer's house regularly. Quote two expressions from paragraphs 1 or 2 which show this.

1. _____

2. _____ **2 1 0**

2. (a) Why do you think the man suggests he will trim the hedge?

_____ **2 ■ 0**

(b) Why does the writer refuse the man's offer to trim the hedge? Answer in your own words.

_____

_____ **2 ■ 0**

3. Look again at paragraph 3. Explain in your own words how other people react to the man with no name.

_____

_____ **2 1 0**

4. What does the word 'understandably' in paragraph 3 tell you about the writer's attitude towards how these people react to the man?

_____

_____ **2 ■ 0**

5. The man 'sleeps rough most of the time'. (paragraph 4) Quote two phrases the writer uses to convey that the places where the man sleeps are unpleasant.

(a) _____

(b) _____ **2 1 0**

		Marks	

6. (a) Why has the writer used inverted commas round the phrase 'unemployed guests wanted'?

_____

_____

2 ■ 0

(b) Why has the writer used inverted commas round the words 'hotels' and 'guest's'

_____

_____

2 ■ 0

7. We are told that 80,000 people are officially homeless in London.

(a) What phrase tells you that the writer does not think this is an accurate number?

[   ]

2 ■ 0

(b) Explain what this phrase means in your own words.

_____

_____

2 1 0

8. In your opinion, why might homelessness make 'a good television story at Christmas or when there is snow or ice'? (paragraph 7)

_____

_____

2 ■ 0

9. Explain in your own words what these phrases tell you about the worries the writer would have about being homeless.
(a) 'uncertainty of the night'

_____

_____

2 1 0

(b) 'fear of the elements'

_____

_____

2 1 0

10. The writer describes the man as 'bearing the familiar scars of homelessness'. (paragraph 9) Explain what ONE of these 'scars' might be, according to the author, quoting to support your answer.

_____

_____

2 1 0

	Marks	

11. The writer offers to take the man to the hospital. In what way is the man's response to this offer 'melodramatic'? (paragraph 9)

_____

_____

| 2 | 1 | 0 |

12. What style of language is used in the phrase 'a few quid'?

_____

_____

| 2 | ■ | 0 |

13. The 'Enterprise Society' (paragraph 10) refers to the Government policy of closing down services that were not profitable. What is the writer's tone in the phrase 'that wonderful expression' and why has he used this tone?

_____

_____

| 2 | 1 | 0 |

14. 'On the common and in the street, he is prey to thugs and to the police' (paragraph 11). Do you find the word 'prey' effective? Give reasons for your answer.

_____

_____

| 2 | 1 | 0 |

15. 'Anyone driving through London's West End knows this to be untrue.' (paragraph 13) Explain fully how this sentence links to the previous paragraph.

_____

_____

| 2 | 1 | 0 |

16. How do European tourists react to the number of homeless people in London? Explain your answer fully, quoting to support your answer.

_____

_____

| 2 | 1 | 0 |

17. (_a_) What is the tourists' attitude to the homeless people in London? Quote from Paragraph 13 to support your answer.

_____

_____

| 2 | 1 | 0 |

(b) What is the French tour guide's attitude to the homeless people in London? Quote to support your answer.

_____

_____

2	1	0

Think about the passage as a whole.

18. 'The Man with No Name' – explain whether you think this is an appropriate title for the article.

_____

_____

2	1	0

19. John Pilger feels very strongly about homelessness. Do you find his writing persuasive? Answer fully, referring to the passage in your answer.

_____

_____

2	1	0

Writing – Foundation/General/Credit

English   Standard Grade: Foundation, General and Credit

Practice Papers
For SQA Exams

Foundation, General and Credit Level
Writing

Read these instructions first.

1. Use the photographs and words to help you think about what to write. Look at it all and consider carefully all possibilities.

2. There are 21 questions to choose from.

3. Decide which **one** you will answer.
   Then write the number is the margin of your answer.

4. Think carefully about the wording of your chosen question.
   Make a **plan** before you start writing.
   Re-read your answer before you finish.
   Mark any changes **neatly**.

Leckie×Leckie
Scotland's leading educational publishers

PRACTICE WRITING PAPER

FIRST   Look at the photograph below. It shows a train leaving a station.

NEXT   Think about going on a journey.

1.   Write about a journey or trip you have made. Remember to include your thoughts and feelings.

2.   Write a short story about a character who makes a train journey. You should develop setting, character and plot.

3.   Write a letter of complaint to a train company about poor service.

FIRST   Look at the photograph below. It shows a baby in a pram.

NEXT   Think about family.

4.   Write about your experience of a new baby in the family. Remember to include your thoughts and feelings.

5.   Over 9000 babies are born each year in Scotland to mothers aged between 13 and 19. Give your views.

6.   'Bringing Up Baby.' Write in any way you like using this title.

FIRST   Look at the picture below. It shows a futuristic city.

NEXT   Think about the future.

7. Write a short story using the following opening:
    He emerged from the time machine and looked out over a strange crystal city he did not recognise. The buildings shone brightly but there was no movement. No life.

8. Write about your hopes and dreams for the future.

9. Mobile phones – a nuisance or an essential piece of technology? Give your views.

10. Write in any way you like about the picture above.

FIRST   Look at the photograph below. It shows a school football match.

NEXT   Think about sporting and leisure activities.

11. Write a letter to your local newspaper to complain about the lack of sporting/leisure facilities in your community.

12. Write a short story about a sporting champion who loses a match/game at a crucial time. You should develop setting, character and plot.

13. The Scottish Government wants to encourage school pupils to be healthy, for example, by providing healthy school dinners and encouraging pupils to take PE. Give your views.

FIRST   Look at the photo below of a busker.

NEXT   Think about different kinds of music.

14. Write a short story about a busker. You should develop setting, character and plot.

15. Write about the music you enjoy and what it means to you.

16. 'Pop is actually my least favourite kind of music because it lacks real depth.' (Christina Aguilera) Give your views.

The following questions do not have any photographs.

17. Zoos are cruel and inhumane. Give your views.

18. 'You've got a friend.' Write in any way you like about friendship.

19. Describe the scene brought to mind by one of the following:
'A full moon hangs, a round, white blaze.'
OR
'Bare branches in winter are a form of writing.'

20. Write a short story in which the main character makes a life-changing decision. You should develop setting and character as well as plot.

21. 'It wasn't us!' Write about an experience you have had when you were part of a group blamed for something.

1. conserve (2)

> *HINT*   Although in this case the answer comes quite early in the paragraph, you should always read the whole paragraph before you decide which word to choose.

TOP EXAM TIP

'One word' means exactly that! Do not try to squeeze other words into the box.

2. magical (1)   beautiful (1)

> *HINT*   The key words in the question are 'positive impression'. You're not being asked just for words which describe the owls, so 'rare' will not do, since that doesn't convey are 'positive impression'. (The word 'touched' *could* possibly be said to create a positive impression of the owls since it shows the effect they have on people who see them, but it is much wiser to go for the obvious choices.)

3. host (2)

> *HINT*   You might be more familiar with 'host' as meaning the person in charge (the host of a party, the host of a game show), but it also means 'a large number' (or an army). Sensible reading of the paragraph shows there's really only one possible answer.

TOP EXAM TIP

When you're looking for a single word you might sometimes have to rely on a common sense 'guess'. (As Sherlock Holmes said: 'When you've eliminated the impossible, whatever remains, however improbable, must be the truth.')

4. unreliable (2)

TOP EXAM TIP

If you're asked to 'find a word that means the same as …' and you can't spot it right away, take the possible answers and see how each of them sounds in place of the given word. This will often make the correct answer obvious.

5. Any two of:
- quite likely
- (we shall) never know
- might have
- may have only

TOP EXAM TIP

When asked for 'an expression', keep it as short as possible – never more than five or six words.

6. Explanation of idea(s) contained in 'mechanisation of farming' and/or 'intensive', eg more machinery was used (1) in the production of food/cultivation of the land (1) which was done in a more focused/rigorous/demanding way (1). [Straight lift: 0]

HINT

After five straightforward questions all of which asked you to quote, all of a sudden you are asked to **explain** something in **your own words**. It is important that you make the shift from quoting to explaining.

For this question, the key words in the passage are 'mechanisation' and 'intensive' and you have to find some way of expressing these ideas in different words. (You have to make it clear to the examiner that you know what these words mean – if you simply quote, then the examiner won't know (and won't give you any marks!).

TOP EXAM TIP

If the question says 'in your own words' you must not simply quote from the passage. It usually means there is a key word or expression for you to find, but in order to show you understand what it means you have to put it into different words.

7. (*a*) To get rid of mice and rats/pests/vermin (2)
   (*b*) It provided shelter (1) and warmth (1)

HINT

There is no stated requirement here to use your own words, but it's always better to try – in fact, here it would be very difficult to answer the question just by quoting. You don't have to find another word for 'mice' or for 'rats', but summarising them as 'pests' or 'vermin' shows really good understanding.

TOP EXAM TIP

If it doesn't say 'in your own words', it is still much wiser to do so. Only if you're specifically told to quote can you do so safely. Certainly, you should never be copying large chunks from the passage.

8. (*a*) Explanation of idea contained in 'drive to be more self-sufficient', e.g. the need to produce as much food as possible (1) in this country/ without having to import (1)

HINT

Notice it's a 2-1-0 question, which suggests there are two ideas being looked for, in this case the need to produce a lot of food and to do so without importing.

TOP EXAM TIP

Remember: 'own words' means find the key words and 'translate' them.

   (*b*) Explanation in own words of any one of the following (2) [Straight lift: 0]:
   'human population expansion'
   'government policies'
   'consumer pressure for ever cheaper food'

HINT

There are actually three reasons – choose the one you find easiest to put into your own words.

9. (*a*) It introduces/gives an expansion/more detail (1) about the 'other factors' (1)
    (*b*) It divides up/separates the items (1) in the list (of other factors) (1)

> **HINT** Remember to describe what the punctuation is doing in *this* paragraph in *this* passage; don't just give a general definition of what the punctuation usually does.

> **TOP EXAM TIP**
> Before the exam, revise the key punctuation marks: comma, colon, semicolon, brackets, dashes, dash, exclamation mark.
> Always be specific when describing what punctuation is doing.

10. (*a*) True (2)
    The first sentence clearly identifies three measures.
    (*b*) False (2)
    False because it says 'most of these can be prevented', i.e. not all.
    (*c*) Can't Tell (2)
    Tricky, but the correct answer is 'Can't Tell' because although we're told that 'Steps can ... be taken to maximise nesting success' and that 'this has been a major part of the Barn Owl Trust's work since 1997', there's no indication about how successful they have been.

> **TOP EXAM TIP**
> Don't agonise too long about 'True/False/Can't Tell' questions. If you think about them too long, you can end up doubting your own judgement!

11. giving advice about owls (2)

> **HINT** The words 'main topic' in the question suggest there are several topics – you have to decide which is the most important. The three 'wrong' answers (called 'distractors' in a multiple-choice question) are not ridiculous – they are all referred to in the paragraph – but the 'main' topic has to be about giving advice.

> **TOP EXAM TIP**
> For this type of question make sure you read the whole paragraph before making your choice. (Try covering up all the options and deciding for yourself what the main topic is.)

12. (*a*) Basic explanation (1) or clear explanation (2) of any one of the following: [Straight lift: 0]:

- 'erect safer nestboxes...'
- 'make alternative provision...'
- '...special floats...'

> **TOP EXAM TIP**
> As with question 8(b), you have three choices – choose the one you find easiest to explain in your own words.

    (*b*) Telling/suggesting opposed to actually doing (2)

> **HINT** Use you understanding of 'practical' from the last question to help you see the difference – one is actually doing things 'hands-on'; the other is telling others what to do.

13. Any two of:
- impressive (track record)
- excellent (reputation)
- highly committed
- very active (volunteers)

HINT   Identify more than two possibilities and then choose the two best.

TOP EXAM TIP

'Expression' – keep it short

14. Making a joke/play on words (1) about birth of organisation using term associated with birds (1)

HINT   Try thinking about the way it would be read out loud. This way you might get some sense of the little joke involved. (Exams might not be the best time to be thinking of humour, but some of the Close Reading passages do contain a little light humour.)

TOP EXAM TIP

As with questions 9(a) and (b), don't just give your standard 'this-is-what-inverted-commas-always-do' answer. In fact, that would not be much use here. Always be alert to what is going on at *this* point in *this* passage.

15. It has brought about positive (1) changes in Local Authority policies (1) [Accept lift]

HINT   'evidence' suggests a specific bit of information; the question is not clear about whether or not to use 'own words' so you should try not to quote (or 'lift') too much. In fact, in this question a lift is acceptable – largely because it would be very difficult to 'translate' the key idea.

16. (A team of) professional staff

HINT   You probably recognise that 'professional' in this context means 'paid' (as in professional footballer or professional musician), so the contrast with 'voluntary' should be obvious.

17. (*a*) Shows the extent/range/large number (1) of the Trust's activities (1)

(*b*) Creates climax (1) to emphasise the importance of the Trust (1)

HINT — You've been told what the features are (often you have to identify them for yourself), so all your effort has to go into describing the effect. Avoid vague answers about what *any* list does – what does *this* list do? Not what *any* delayed subject does, but what does *this* delayed subject do? Notice that in both answers you must refer to the work of the Barn Owl Trust.

TOP EXAM TIP

When answering on Sentence Structure, never lose sight of **meaning** – what's going on in *this* sentence in *this* passage.

18. (i) Accept either; no marks for choice

(ii) One appropriate specific reference in support of choice (1)

Two appropriate specific references in support of choice **or** an appropriate general overview of the passage (2)

HINT — Questions about 'the Passage as a whole' can be a bit scary, but don't be put off by them. No one is asking you do anything impossible. Read the question very carefully and do exactly what you're told to do. Your opinion is important. No one is going to say your opinion is wrong – you will be marked according to how well you support your opinion.

TOP EXAM TIP

Try looking at the last question before you start on any of the questions! The last question often asks you to 'think about the passage as a whole', so if you know at the beginning what it is you'll have to know about the whole passage, you might be able to think about it while you are answering the other questions. This way you will maybe have some good ideas for the last question without having to read the whole passage again.

PRACTICE EXAM A   CREDIT LEVEL WORKED ANSWERS

1. Reference to or explanation of any three of:
- Harris has 'long disappeared'
- only water ahead
- most remote part
- sits alone

3 points = 2; 2 points = 1; 1 point = 0

HINT — Be careful not to pick just any descriptive detail. Key words in this question are 'sense of isolation' – make sure your choices connect with that. For example, the description of the spray and the smirr is quite impressive, but it hasn't got anything to do with 'isolation'.

TOP EXAM TIP

'Give' in the question usually means you can quote.

2. Cluster of islands (2)

HINT 'earlier in the passage' tells you the answer is in paragraph 1 or 2. If you know what an 'archipelago' is, this question will be very easy; if you don't, use common sense to see that it must be a way of describing the islands.

TOP EXAM TIP

'expression' is a short group of words – rarely more than five in total.

3. They will be working (1)/unpaid (1)/doing menial tasks (1) – any two

HINT A straightforward Understanding question, but one which needs you to look at the details *before* the quotation in the question.

Notice how 'menial tasks' in the answer is a good way to show understanding of all the items in the list of jobs.

TOP EXAM TIP

Notice this question asks for 'ways' (plural), so you should make sure there are (at least) two ideas in your answer.

This question doesn't ask specifically for 'own words', but it is always best to try. In this case, simply quoting 'the volunteers ... clearing drains' will not show any *understanding*.

4. Natural: reference to landscape and/or wildlife (2)
Cultural: reference to history/tradition/way of life etc (2)

HINT Notice that both parts are for 2 or 0 marks; in other words there is a single key idea required – as the answer shows clearly

TOP EXAM TIP

For this type of question there will usually be lots of help in the passage. In this case there is plenty reference in paragraph 4 (and you should read the whole paragraph *before* answering question 4) to history and lifestyle as well as to wildlife and landscape.

5. Gloss on any two of:
- 'struggling to survive'
- 'numbers had dwindled'
- 'life…becoming increasingly harsh'

Lifts: 0

HINT Remember to look before and after the idea referred to in the question. In this case the answer comes *after*.

Notice that the answer asks for a 'gloss' – this is examiner-speak for an explanation in different words.

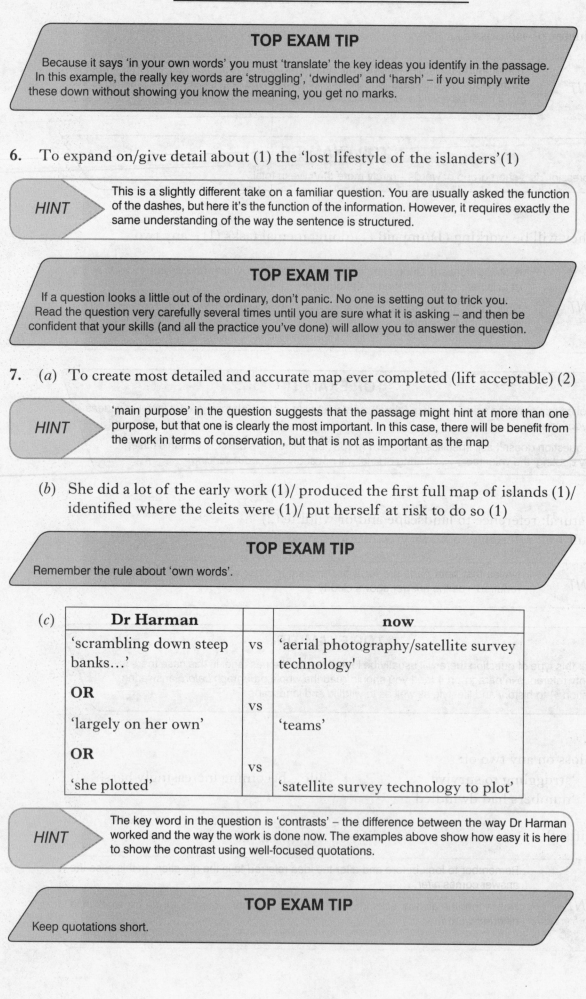

TOP EXAM TIP

Because it says 'in your own words' you must 'translate' the key ideas you identify in the passage. In this example, the really key words are 'struggling', 'dwindled' and 'harsh' – if you simply write these down without showing you know the meaning, you get no marks.

6. To expand on/give detail about (1) the 'lost lifestyle of the islanders'(1)

HINT This is a slightly different take on a familiar question. You are usually asked the function of the dashes, but here it's the function of the information. However, it requires exactly the same understanding of the way the sentence is structured.

TOP EXAM TIP

If a question looks a little out of the ordinary, don't panic. No one is setting out to trick you. Read the question very carefully several times until you are sure what it is asking – and then be confident that your skills (and all the practice you've done) will allow you to answer the question.

7. (*a*) To create most detailed and accurate map ever completed (lift acceptable) (2)

HINT 'main purpose' in the question suggests that the passage might hint at more than one purpose, but that one is clearly the most important. In this case, there will be benefit from the work in terms of conservation, but that is not as important as the map

(*b*) She did a lot of the early work (1)/ produced the first full map of islands (1)/ identified where the cleits were (1)/ put herself at risk to do so (1)

TOP EXAM TIP

Remember the rule about 'own words'.

(*c*)

Dr Harman		now
'scrambling down steep banks…'	vs	'aerial photography/satellite survey technology'
OR		
'largely on her own'	vs	'teams'
OR		
'she plotted'	vs	'satellite survey technology to plot'

HINT The key word in the question is 'contrasts' – the difference between the way Dr Harman worked and the way the work is done now. The examples above show how easy it is here to show the contrast using well-focused quotations.

TOP EXAM TIP

Keep quotations short.

8. Some understanding of 'mystique' (1) + reference to the obscurity of their purpose (1)

> *HINT* — Notice that the answer requires you to show you know what 'mystique' means. You might think this is unfair since it is not directly said in the question. However, unless you know what it means you can't *really* show how the cleits add to it!

TOP EXAM TIP

Note that it's 'way' (singular) but it's a 2-1-0 question, so there must be two elements to the answer, as the answer here demonstrates clearly.

9. **Word choice:**
- 'Suddenly'(1) – sense of surprise, etc (1)
- 'greyness' (1) – sense of mystery, threat, etc (1)
- 'sheer' (1) – sense of danger, etc (1)
- 'rise' (1) – (personification) suggests something slightly threatening, sinister, etc
- 'swirling' (1) – sense of rapid movement (1)
- '(more than) half a million' – sense of enormous numbers, etc (1)

> *HINT* — Make sure you read to the end of the question. In this case you get an important signpost right at the end: 'make this paragraph dramatic', so you need to direct your comments towards this idea.

TOP EXAM TIP

When dealing with Word Choice, always try to say what the word suggests. Look at all the possibilities above and see how it can be done.

Sentence Structure:
- short sentences (1) – abrupt, mysterious, etc (1)
- delayed subject ('… St Kilda appears.') – ominous, menacing, etc (1)
- parenthetical 'the largest colony in Europe' – explains/emphasises the surprising uniqueness of the place (1)

> *HINT* — Make sure you read to the end of the question. In this case you get an important signpost right at the end: 'make this paragraph dramatic', so you need to direct your comments towards this.

TOP EXAM TIP

When dealing with Sentence Structure (which most people find difficult – even when they get to Higher), always try to describe the *effect* or *impact* of the sentence structure feature. Look at all the possibilities above and see how it can be done.

10. (i)   Gloss on 'far exceed' (1) 'what the islands themselves deliver' (1) [Lifts: 0]

(ii)   Gloss on 'they fail to capture' (1) 'its unique atmosphere' (1) [Lifts: 0]

TOP EXAM TIP

Remember 'own words'. This question refers to a very small part of the passage, but there are four marks available, so there's a lot at stake.

11. In a neutral way (2)

 If you don't actually know the meaning, try to work it out from the context. If you're still stuck eliminate the unlikely ones and if necessary, make a reasonable guess.

12. It is not a village in the normal sense of the word (2)/some people might call it a village but the writer doesn't agree (2)

TOP EXAM TIP

When asked about features such as inverted commas, remember to give an answer specific to *these* inverted commas in *this* passage – not just a general comment which could apply to *any* inverted commas.

13. (i)   Eerie: chilling/creepy/strange (1) to be reminded of people no longer here (1)

(ii)   Comforting: reassuring/soothing/cheering (1) that they are remembered OR that there is something personal in such a bleak setting (1)

HINT Questions about 'feelings' will require a little reading between the lines. In this case think about the situation: deserted village, roofless houses, visitor (writer) seeing names of former occupants. What will she be thinking?

TOP EXAM TIP

In questions about feelings or emotions, try to put yourself in the mind of the writer or the character.

14. (*a*)   Because a military base does not fit in (1) with the idyllic/peaceful/relaxing notion that people have of the islands (1)

(*b*)   It is part of the island (1) and it would be false to pretend it doesn't exist. (1)

 Simple enough questions, but you need to work out (or know) what 'cropped' means. It refers to the process of 'doctoring' a photograph by not including bits from one or more of the edges.

15. Any two of the following:
- 'different sizes' (1) – makes it difficult to be precise about purpose (1)
- 'mythology' (1) – links them with magical tales of old (1)
- 'unique' (1) – there is nothing like them anywhere (1)
- 'something like igloos' (1) – not possible to give exact description (1)
- 'most likely' (1) – element of uncertainty (1)
- 'large enough for ten people' (1) – no indication of purpose (1)
- 'only a child' (1) – something this small seems pointless (1)

TOP EXAM TIP

Remember the instruction 'By referring … explain' i.e. two things to be done in each answer. Be methodical. Study the list of possibilities above.

16. Any three of:
- 'piercing blue'
- 'glide and circle'
- 'sparkles in the sunlight'
- 'needlepoints'
- 'rise high and proud'

TOP EXAM TIP

When a question asks for three short quotes like this, it is very likely that there are maybe four or five possibilities. Try to identify more than you need and then choose the best three.

17. Your comments should be about the atmosphere (bleak, isolated, extremes of dark/silence, surrounded by nature, etc) (1) with at least one appropriate reference. (1)

HINT

When you read Paragraph 12 carefully you should become aware that it is mostly concerned with describing the mood or atmosphere. To discuss whether or not this is an effective way to end the passage, think back to earlier parts of the passage where the writer focuses on atmosphere, e.g. Paragraphs 1 (isolation), 7 (natural beauty), 10 (mystery).

There are several specific details in the paragraph you could use: 'trample', 'like a mouth gulping in the ocean', 'the end of a stone pier', 'inky black', 'shiny waves', 'the wind whips around'. What could you say about each of these? How could you relate it to the passage as a whole?

TOP EXAM TIP

Questions about 'the Passage as a whole' can be intimidating, but don't be frightened by them. No one is asking you do anything impossible. Read them carefully and do exactly what you're told to do. Your opinion is important. No one is going to say your opinion is wrong – you will be marked according to how well you support your opinion

1. He remembered being an outsider (2)

OR

He remembered nothing except being an outsider (2)

HINT

> Usually, the first question is not too difficult. This question asks you to explain the second sentence in the paragraph; 'Daniel had no memories other than of being an outsider'.

2. It was his birthday (1) and it was his first day at school (1)

HINT

> Some pupils find it helpful to underline key words in the questions to help them to focus on what is being looked for. In this question, the key phrase is the date '3ʳᵈ of March 1767' and the key word is 'important'. So you know that you are looking for information about that date – which is found easily in paragraph 2.

TOP EXAM TIP

Questions will usually follow the order of the passage. So, the first questions will usually ask you about the first few sentences or paragraphs of the passage. Then the questions will work through the passage chronologically (in order that the events happened). Examiners write questions in this way to make things easier for you – so you will not have to 'jump around' the passage to find the answers you are looking for!

3. He did not answer when asked to read a simple word (2)

OR

The teacher thought he could not read (2)

OR

He did not know/understand what the teacher wanted him to do (2)

HINT

> Again, it may be helpful to underline key words in the questions to help you to focus on what is being looked for. In this question, the key phrase is 'the teachers… thought' and the key word is 'stupid'. So you know that you are looking for information about the teachers at the school and for an example of something Daniel did which the teachers might have thought was stupid.

TOP EXAM TIP

This is what we call an 'understanding' question – these ask you to explain ideas in the passage. Question 1 was also an 'understanding' question.

In question 2, you are asked to explain in your own words so there is no need to quote. And sometimes you are asked to quote so there is no need to use your own words! If you are ever not sure whether to quote or use your own words, do both.

4. She spanked/beat/hit him (2)

> The key word in the question is 'reacted' – in other words, how did Mrs Bartholemew behave when Daniel did not answer. Find the sentence in the passage where the teacher shows him the engraving. The answer is actually four sentences later.

5. Daniel was more interested in... concentrating on his own special numbers (2)
OR
Multiplication tables were too easy for Daniel (2)

> In the passage, find the sentence which tells you that Daniel was not interested in multiplication. Did you spot it? The answer is in the next sentence.

TOP EXAM TIP

You will often be asked about an idea in the passage but you have to answer 'in your own words'. Many pupils answer these questions by quoting the exact words from the passage. You will not be given any marks for doing this. For example, if you had written for this answer 'he was collecting his special numbers' or 'he was looking under the desk' you would be given no marks as you have simply copied these phrases from the passage.

6. He was lonely/alone/on his own/friendless/a loner (2)

> This question is easy if you know the meaning of the word 'solitary' which means alone. If you did not know this, could you have made a guess based on what you have learned about Daniel from the passage? It's also always worth checking the glossary in case a definition is given there, as it is in this case. If you are not sure of an answer, think about it but don't spend too long on it. If you are really stuck, leave it and come back to it when you have finished the rest of the questions. Sometimes, just working through other questions and answers will help you in understanding the passage – and can mean you finally 'get' that difficult question!

TOP EXAM TIP

Did you notice that you did not have to make two points in your answer this time – even though the question is worth two marks? Sometimes, examiners give two marks for an answer to a difficult question. This can make it tricky sometimes to work out how much to write, but working through this book will help you. If you do not give the correct answer you will be given 0 marks.

7. She 'pounced' (1) on him meaning that she swooped down/jumped on him suddenly (1).
OR
She suddenly grabbed/pulled with force/grasped (1) the notebook; this is shown by the word 'seized' (1)

> You are being asked here to explain and quote from the passage. Look at the two suggested answers again – the first answer quotes first then explains. The second answer explains then quotes. Try answering in both ways and find out which order you prefer.

8. She was interested/intrigued/concerned/angry/wanted to know more about what was in the notebook/his ability in Maths (1)
    AND
    She took it to look at later/show to someone else/so he could not look at it in class (1)

> **HINT**
>
> This question asks for your opinion – the key phrase in the question is 'Why do you think...'.
>
> Of course, your answer must be based on your understanding of the passage – as well as your general knowledge. In this case, you can probably work out that the teacher felt an emotion when she looked at the book – concern, anger, curiosity? She wanted to know more about what was in the notebook (remember that earlier in the passage, you read that it had special numbers in it) and you can guess that she might want to show it to someone else/another teacher/look at it again later for herself.

9. He wanted it back because it was special to him/belonged to him (1); we are told it was 'precious' (1)
    OR
    He did not need it back because the numbers were 'in his head' (1)– he knew them off by heart/for himself (1)

> **HINT**
>
> You are being asked here to answer in your own words and support your opinion by using evidence from the passage. Look at the two suggested answers again – the first answer quotes from the passage first then explains. The second answer explains then quotes. Try answering in both ways and find out which order you prefer.

> **TOP EXAM TIP**
>
> Examiners use different ways of asking you to quote from the passage in an answer.
>
> Look at the phrases below and get to know them – they are all asking you to refer back to the passage and quote!
>
> - *Quote from the passage...*
> - *Which word/phrase...?*
> - *Give an example...*
> - *Refer closely to the passage...*
> - *Identify the word(s)...*
> - *Write down the word(s)...*
> - *What expression...?*

10. Daniel was clean and smart (1)
    OR
    His sisters had been taken out of the house/sent away (1)
    OR
    His parents were waiting anxiously (1)
    OR
    They were waiting in the parlour (1)
    OR
    Daniel's parents did not show any emotion (1)

> **TOP EXAM TIP**
>
> Always 'have a go' at a question. You may feel you have no idea what the answer is but if you write nothing, you will gain no marks! If you write an answer, you just might be correct so never leave an answer blank.

11. He ran to his room and fetched a grid with numbers (1)
AND/OR
He discussed the numbers with Dr Adair excitedly (1)
AND/OR
He shared his book with Dr Adair (1)
AND/OR
He asked Dr Adair for something (1)

HINT To answer this question correctly, you need to work out the meaning of 'in awe'. If you know this phrase means 'in admiration' or 'showing great respect', well done! When you do not know the meaning of a word or phrase, try to work out the meaning by looking at the other words and phrases AROUND it. You are then looking for something that Daniel does which shows us that he behaved normally and NOT formally or by being overpolite. You get one mark for each point you make up to a maximum of two.

12. This is a long sentence with several phrases/divided by commas (1) which reflects/copies/sounds like how Daniel was speaking (1).

HINT This is an 'analysis' question that asks you to think about the writer's craft. In other words, you are being asked about HOW the writer has placed the words in this sentence (and why).

Any question which asks you about word choice or sentence structure is an 'analysis' question.

When answering analysis questions, many pupils only explain WHAT the sentence means. You should explain what it means <u>and</u> write about the structure or word choice to have a chance of full marks.

In this question you are asked about what is unusual in the sentence structure. Here it is used to look and sound like the boy's actual speech.

TOP EXAM TIP

In sentence structure questions, you should comment on

how the writer has chosen to punctuate the sentence

and/or

how long or short the sentence is and why

and/or

the pattern of the sentence and why it has been written in this way

13. His father was embarrassed by Daniel. (2)

HINT You are being asked here to work out the meaning of the phrase 'exposing his oddness to a stranger'. The word 'oddness' means strangeness – if the father thinks his son is behaving strangely in front of a stranger then his feeling is most likely to be embarrassment.

14. His friend will be interested because the grid has been done by such a young child. (2)

OR

His friend will be interested because it 'was created by a boy of seven'. (2)

> **HINT**
>
> This question asks for your opinion – the key phrase in the question is 'Why do you think…'.
>
> Your answer must be based on your understanding of the passage – as well as your general knowledge. In this case, you can probably work out that Dr Adair is surprised or impressed by Daniel's ability in Maths at such a young age.

TOP EXAM TIP

Did you notice that you can gain either two mark or zero marks for your answer here? As in Question 6, you will be given two marks for making only one point.

15. She uses 'he' instead of 'you' (1)

AND/OR

She uses informal, slangy language – 'don't he' (1).

AND/OR

Dr Adair uses formal, polite language (1).

AND/OR

Dr Adair uses a long sentence/she uses a short sentence (1).

AND/OR

Dr Adair uses complex words such as 'acquaintance' (1).

> **HINT**
>
> This is another analysis question – you are being asked about HOW the woman speaks to Daniel – not WHAT she says to him. Did you notice that the answer contains quotes from what she says?
>
> It is important to be able to tell the difference between formal and informal language. Informal (sometimes called 'colloquial' or 'conversational') language is everyday, slangy language, for example, the kind of words you use in the playground or with your friends. Formal language is used for writing and when you are in a formal situation e.g. a job interview, writing a school essay etc.
>
> | Formal | Informal |
> | --- | --- |
> | No slang | Slang |
> | Fewer or no abbreviations | Abbreviations (e.g. isn't instead of 'is not') |
> | Complex sentences | Simple sentences |
> | Complex words | Simple words |
>
> You gain one mark for each difference, up to a maximum of two.

16. It meant little/nothing to him/it was meaningless (1)
AND/OR
He thought it would be quite like/the same as dame school (1)
AND/OR
He was happy to go to the Academy (1) (no marks for 'blithely')
AND/OR
He was not concerned or worried about the Academy (1)

17. A boy or boys at the school (1)

Because he or they thought Daniel's father's job was unimportant or inferior or embarrassing (1)

TOP EXAM TIP

Looking at the ideas before and after the quote you have been given will help you to find the answer – 'other boys' are mentioned at the beginning of the paragraph and the phrase 'A boy took everything...' follows the quotation.

18. Other pupils laughed at his father's job/position (1).
AND/OR
A boy threw all Daniel's clothes out of the window into the mud (1).
AND/OR
A teacher pulled his ear/caned him for saying he had not thrown the clothes out (1).
AND/OR
A big boy lifted him onto a wall and pushed/prodded him until he had to jump off.

19. (a) He felt comfortable/secure there/it 'fitted' him/it was unusual like him (2)
(b) He felt empty/emotionless/miserable (2)

20. 'a journey between one world and another' (2)

TOP EXAM TIP

The key word 'between' helps you here – between 'one world' (Daniel's home) and 'another' world (Daniel's school).

21. They were proud and pleased that he was attending the Academy (2)

HINT To answer this question, you have to find the key phrase in the passage which means explaining his true feelings – 'he could not tell them how he felt'. The answer is found BEFORE this phrase at the beginning of the sentence – 'His mother and father were so proud....'

22. (a) Metaphor or imagery (2)

HINT Another analysis question which asks you about the writer's word choice. Did you spot that 'anchored' is a metaphor? Sometimes you will be told that you are analysing a metaphor or simile but – more likely – you will be asked to identify the technique just as you are in this question. Of course, you have to spot that this is an image or specifically, a metaphor!

(b) 'Anchored' tells us that he feels secure/supported/safe at home (2).

TOP EXAM TIP

Writers use a number of techniques and you could be asked about any of them. Make sure you can recognise:

- imagery (metaphors or similes or personification)
- onomatopoeia
- alliteration

23. This is an effective opening because the writer tells us a lot of detail about the character of Daniel. For example, the writer describes Daniel's ability in Maths; ('his special numbers') and Daniel's personality ('being out of step with the world'). (2)

OR

This is an effective opening because it describes how Daniel is an 'outsider'. For example, how his ability in Maths sets him apart from others and how he is bullied at the Naval Academy because of his 'oddness'. (2)

HINT

To gain the full two marks here, you should give a full and clear explanation making at least two points as well as stating whether you think the opening is effective or not.

The answers given here are examples of how you might answer this question. As always with 'evaluation' questions, base your answer on the passage but include your own opinions. Of course, you could say that you do not think the opening is effective – as long as you can justify your answer with evidence from the passage.

Whatever reasons you give, make sure you use quotes to back up your answer.

PRACTICE EXAM B   CREDIT LEVEL WORKED ANSWERS

1. (a) He did not enjoy it AND says it is 'dreary' (2)

OR

It is dull/ boring/poorly written/a waste of time (2)

OR

He did not enjoy the experience of reading it/did not think it was worth reading (2)

HINT

Usually, the first question is not too difficult! Some pupils find it helpful to underline key words in the questions to help them to focus on what is being looked for. In this question, the key word is 'feel'. So you know that you are looking for Dixon's <u>emotion</u> or <u>attitude</u> towards the novel.

TOP EXAM TIP

This is what we call an 'understanding' question – an 'understanding' question asks you to explain ideas in the passage. You should answer the question by quoting from the passage and then explaining the quote in your own words. Sometimes, you are asked to explain in your own words so there is no need to quote. And sometimes you are asked to quote so there is no need to use your own words! If you are ever in doubt about whether to quote or use your own words, do both...

(*b*) 'kill a few hours in reading' (1)

TOP EXAM TIP

If you are asked for a word or short phrase from the passage, there is usually an empty box on the answer sheet. Write the word or phrase inside the box – remembering to use quotation marks and to quote exactly as the words are used in the passage.

2. The weather was bad/poor (1) so she may have wanted to be on her own as she was feeling unwell/seasick (1).
    OR
    She may have wanted to be on her own to be away from Dixon (1) as she had wanted to be on her own since the voyage began (1).
    OR
    She was annoyed at Dixon (1) and did not want to be on the ship (1).

 **HINT** This is another 'understanding 'question but this time you are asked to answer in your own words. So you will get no marks for quoting!

3. The morning had been calm (1).
    AND/OR
    It started with only a single drop of rain (1).
    AND/OR
    It became heavy within five minutes/very quickly (1).

 HINT This is another 'understanding 'question – as you are not asked to answer in your own words, it is acceptable to quote directly from the passage in your answer.

However, finding an answer can be difficult. In this question, the key word is 'surprise'. But the word 'surprise' does not occur in the paragraph you are looking at! You have to think more deeply and work out what aspects of the weather or the storm meant it came as a shock. Common sense tells you that this might be because it happened quickly or unexpectedly.

4. The captain/a senior member of the crew (1)

    After the instruction, we are told 'The sailors were already running' (1).

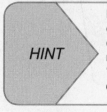 **HINT** This is another 'understanding 'question – you are not asked to answer in your own words, so it is acceptable to quote directly from the passage in your answer.

We are not told directly who said these words. You have to look after the instruction to find out who carried it out. This helps you to work out who is speaking to whom!

5. 'vibrations' (2)

HINT Here is the best technique if you are asked for the meaning of a word (or phrase) you do not know. Look at the <u>context</u> of the word because the context may contain words or phrases that have a similar meaning or may help you work out the meaning. Context means the words and phrases round about the word or phrase itself. So the phrases 'a powerful gust buffeted' and 'shattering crockery' may give you a clue that the wind caused the reverberations or vibrations of the mast which in turn made the china break.

6. 'a lurch' and 'a sway' are separated by semi colons (1) and this reflects the jerky/ side to side movement of the ship (1)

HINT

Examiners often include questions on sentence structure at Credit level. These can be called 'analysis' questions – questions which ask you to analyse the writer's craft. In other words, you will be asked about the choices the writer has made about structure and language.

When answering, many pupils only explain what the sentence <u>means</u>. You should explain what it means <u>and</u> comment on the structure or word choice <u>and</u> why it has been used or is effective to gain full marks.

TOP EXAM TIP

In sentence structure questions, you should comment on

- how the writer has chosen to punctuate the sentence or
- how long or short the sentence is and why or
- the pattern of the sentence and why it has been written in this way

To gain full marks, you have to comment on the <u>effect</u> of the punctuation, length or pattern; in other words, what the structure <u>does</u>. Here it <u>reflects</u> or <u>copies</u> the ship's movement.

7. The writer's word choice is effective as he uses the word 'music' to describe the sounds of the ship (1), for example, 'rumbles', 'clatter', 'clank', 'groaning' (1), which help to build up a detailed picture of the scene.

HINT

For full marks, you have to identify that 'music' is referring to the sounds the ship was making. The sounds are all described in the lines following. This is why you are asked to refer to these lines. You also have to quote examples of these words.

TOP EXAM TIP: CREDIT

There will always be several questions about word choice at Credit level.
In word choice questions, you should comment on:

- the specific words the writer has used and
- the effect of these words on the reader

To gain full marks, quote the words, explain them in your own words and then analyse the effect they create.

TOP EXAM TIP

Examiners use different ways to ask you to quote from the passage. Did you notice in this question you are asked to 'comment on the word choice'? This is one way of asking you to quote.
Look at the phrases below and get to know them – they are all asking you to quote!

- Support your answer with evidence…
- Quote from the passage…
- Using evidence…
- Give an example…
- Illustrate your answer (This does not mean draw a picture!)…
- Refer closely to… / by close reference to…
- Identify the word(s)…
- Write down the word(s)…
- What expression…?

8. This image (1) is effective because the wave is very powerful/violent and a punch is also powerful/violent (1). This image is effective because it emphasises the strength/force of the wave. (1)

HINT

This is an example of a question which asks you to analyse but also asks for your opinion, too. You are asked if you think the image is effective. You can say it is or is not effective as long as you give good clear reasons for your answer.

Did you notice there are 2 marks available here? You should identify, the properties of the wave for 1 mark, and comment on why it is effective for the second mark.

Remember whenever you are asked to explain an image you should

- identify what two things/people are being compared
- state whether you think this is an effective comparison and why

TOP EXAM TIP

At Credit level, you should expect a question about imagery, for example,

- simile or
- metaphor or
- personification

You may be given the image or you may have to find it for yourself. You then have to comment on how effective it is. A technique some pupils find helpful is to list as many similarities as possible between the object/movement/action/feeling itself and the object/movement/action/feeling to which it is compared. The more similarities, the more effective the image!

9. The writer creates an atmosphere of tension (1) through the use of verbs which suggest force or extreme movement (1) e.g. snapped, shattering, violently (1)
OR
the use of present tense verbs (1) e.g. surging, crumpling, roaring (1)
OR
description of the passengers' reactions (1) e.g. 'terrified screams', 'bellow' (1)
OR
imagery that emphasises the strength of the wave (1) e.g. 'a battlement', 'like a mace' (1)
OR
sentence structure (1) e.g. one-word sentences or non-sentences, e.g. 'A hail of cups and splintering plates.' (1)

As you can see from the example answers here, you will gain one mark for identifying a technique and one mark for quoting correctly an example of this technique.

HINT

You will often be asked in the Credit paper about mood or atmosphere. Practise reading different types of fiction texts and working out the mood. Remember that mood can be created through a number of different techniques including

- word choice
- imagery
- sentence structure/length

10. (*a*) clamour (1)
    (*b*) bellow (1)

11. 'skreek' is an onomatopoeic word (1) which mimics or copies or reflects or sounds like the sound of metal on metal (1).
    OR
    'skreek' is an onomatopoeic word (1) which mimics or copies or reflects or sounds like scratch/squeak/screech (1).

> **HINT**
>
> Another analysis question which asks you about onomatopoeia. You have to be able to identify when onomatopoeia is being used and, in addition, be able to explain what the word (s) convey/add/show.
>
> What other onomatopoeic words do you know?

12. The man had a club foot (1)
    OR
    She was hysterical(1)
    OR
    It was wet/slippy(1)
    OR
    She could not hold on(1)

13. (*a*) I do not find these instructions convincing as they suggest everyone is safe/ should not panic/this is a regular occurrence (1) which contrasts with the description of the violence and force of the storm (1).

    (*b*) The Captain (1) has told them to remain on a lower level/lower deck (1)

> **HINT**
>
> In the first part of this question, you have to find the instructions and then say if you find them convincing. It is tricky to find the instructions themselves as they are written as reported speech. This means the instructions are not written as the actual words the stewards said using speech marks or inverted commas. This reported speech starts at 'Passengers were to retire' up to 'everyone to remain below', eight sentences in total.
>
> Now for your opinion – put yourself in the position of one of the passengers. Having read up to this point, would you be reassured by these instructions? Note in the answer above that the pupil clearly writes his or her own opinion using 'I do not...' You could also use phrases such as
>
> - in my opinion
> - my evaluation is
> - I feel
> - I think
> - my view of
>
> In the second part of the question, you are asked to find who sends a message that contradicts this. This word means 'to oppose' or to state the opposite view. So you know that you are looking for an instruction that suggests the passengers are in danger or that there is need for concern.

TOP EXAM TIP

Questions that ask for your opinion can be called 'evaluation' questions. In other words, you are being asked to make a judgement. Here you are asked if the instructions were convincing.

Your opinion is never wrong – so it is OK to agree or disagree! Don't forget, though, that you have to back up your opinion with reasons – also called 'evidence'. Remember that when you see the word 'evidence' in a Close Reading question, this means you have to quote or explain ideas from the passage. Only use evidence you have from other reading or knowledge or experience if you are specifically asked for this.

14. The speaker is angry/impatient/annoyed (1). This is conveyed by the use of an exclamation/by the use of commands (1).

HINT

This is another analysis question so you should
- identify the emotion
- identify an aspect of language that tells you this

As with all analysis questions, you are being asked about HOW the writer has used language and not what it means! So you would gain no marks for answering 'The speaker tells everyone to go inside'.

15. Any three from
- 'peopled by puppets'
- 'show off gushiness'
- 'strained for its effects'
- 'crushed by the weight of its prose style'
- 'an attempt'
- 'over-ambitious'
- 'stagger into weary life'
- 'like trudging through a peatbog'

TOP EXAM TIP

Sometimes it is tricky to work out how marks are allocated! Here you are asked for three criticisms but there is a maximum of two marks. It works like this
- three criticisms correct = 2 marks
- two criticisms correct = 1 mark
- one criticism correct = 0 marks

16. The language is melodramatic/exaggerated/dramatic (1); for example, the repetition of the phrase 'the more … the more …'
OR
'I have no pity' or the use of exaggerated images such as 'worms writhing' (1)
OR
'crush out their entrails'
OR
the exclamation marks (1).

TOP EXAM TIP

The phrase 'comment fully' in the question tells you to write more than one brief point in your answer. You can see that there are two marks here – one for identifying the style of language and one for quoting examples of this.

17. (a) Dixon feels his novel is well organised (1) in contrast to the minister's (1)

 (b) Rhetorical question (2) or exaggeration/hyperbole (2) or imagery, e.g. 'sludge'(2)

HINT	Note that you should not quote the phrase 'carefully constructed' as you are asked to answer in your own words.
	You can use formal terminology for language effects such as 'hyperbole' but you do not need to know this. You can use the more usual term 'exaggeration'. The important thing is to be able to identify these kinds of effects.

18. 'yet' means despite, however, but (1)
 OR
 'yet' links back to the previous paragraph (1)
 AND
 'yet' introduces a contrasting idea (1)
 OR
 Laura loves the novel whereas he hates it as described in the previous paragraph (1).

TOP EXAM TIP

In this answer, you should explain what the linking word 'yet' does – it introduces an opposing or contrasting idea (conveyed in the paragraph before). Then you have to explain this contrasting idea – that Laura loves the novel and Dixon hates it.

TOP EXAM TIP: CREDIT

You may be asked at Credit level to explain the function of a word, phrase or sentence. For example, you could be asked about the function of a sentence at the beginning or at the end of a paragraph, sometimes called a topic sentence.

Often, the function of a sentence is to link – either with ideas before it or after it. There is usually a key word or phrase which 'signals' the function to you.

The function of a word or phrase can be to 'signal' added information, a summary, an explanation, to show a result, to contrast.

Look at the linking words and phrases below – can you work out their functions?

• in short
• furthermore
• the former ... the latter ...
• besides
• since
• as a result
• nonetheless
• unlike

19. She would like the novel he is reading whereas he hates it (1) OR she babbles or chatters meaninglessly (1) OR she had said she liked his novel but had not meant this (1)

HINT

Remember that you are looking for ideas either AFTER or BEFORE the key phrase you are given. In fact, for this answer, the reasons Dixon hates his wife are placed <u>before</u> the key phrase you have been given. You will usually be directed to where to look, for example, 'Read paragraph 4 again...' or 'In Line 24....'. At Credit level, however, you may be expected to find an answer without being directed to where the answer is – as in Question 12.

20. He is very successful as the passage describes so many unpleasant aspects of being on board; for example, the physical danger of being at sea in a storm or the basic rations or the boredom. (2)

TOP EXAM TIP

At Credit level, you may be asked to 'judge' the success of a writer. You may feel he is not successful, fairly successful (perhaps some aspects are convincing and others are not) or very successful. Answer according to your opinion but always include plenty of evidence from the text to back up your answer.

21. (*a*) Grantley Dixon

I do not feel sympathetic towards Dixon. He has a high opinion of his writing ability, despite his novel being rejected and he is rude about other people's writing. He also does not seem caring or respectful towards his wife – for example, he describes her behaviour as 'laughable'. (2)

(*b*) Laura Dixon

I feel sympathy towards Laura Dixon as her husband seems to be interested only in himself, for example, reading frequently. She is also frightened by the storm but is not comforted by Dixon – in fact, she is 'grabbed by an angry faced Merredith' but Dixon still doesn't go to her. (2)

TOP EXAM TIP

The final question in the Credit Close Reading is usually an evaluation question – one which asks for your opinion on as aspect of the passage. In this case, you are asked about the characters the writer has created.
In your answer, you should

• express your opinion (you either sympathise or do not sympathise)
• explain your reasons for this in your own words
• refer to the text and/or quote from the text

There are other reasons for sympathising with these characters that are not included here. The important thing to remember here is that sympathy – or lack of it – must be based on something the writer has conveyed about the character. Don't forget that 'by close reference' means you have to quote and/or comment closely on words/ideas in the text.

1. (*a*) In 1950, pork was the most widely eaten/popular meat (1) but, by 1970, Americans were eating twice as much beef as pork (1).

> *HINT*
>
> Questions will usually follow the order of the passage. So the first questions will usually ask you about the first few sentences or paragraphs of the passage. Then the questions will work through the passage is the passage's order. Examiners write questions in this way to make things easier for you – so you will not have to 'jump around' to find the answers you are looking for!

TOP EXAM TIP

Usually, the first question is not too difficult. Some pupils find it helpful to underline key words in the questions to help them to focus on what is being looked for. In this question, the key word is 'changed'. So you know that you are looking for information about the American Diet **changing** between 1950 and 1970. You will gain only one mark for making a point about the American diet in 1950 and only one mark for making a point about the change in the American diet by 1970. You need to make **both** points to gain two marks.

   (*b*) McDonalds (1)
      'one company more than any other '(1)

2. The story of how McDonald's started gives only the company's version of what happened, which the author distrusts (2).
   OR
   The writer does not believe/is suspicious of the story told by McDonald's about how it started (2).
   OR
   The story McDonald's tells about how it started may not be the truth – the writer is doubtful about the official company story (2).

TOP EXAM TIP

This question asks you about the writer's attitude or opinion towards the subject he is writing about. You can work out the writer's attitude or opinion from the words and ideas the writer uses. The word 'conveyed' means 'communicated' or 'told'. Did you work out that the writer might feel distrustful or suspicious about what the company has said about itself? You will gain **one** mark for making the point that there is a McDonald's 'version' of how the company started. Your **second** mark is for explaining how the writer feels about this.

3. He was a salesman for Multimixers and wondered why the hamburger stand needed so many Multimixers (2).
   OR
   He was surprised by how many/the large number of Multimixers the stand used (2).

TOP EXAM TIP

This is what we call an 'understanding' question – these ask you to explain ideas or information in the passage. Question 1 was also an 'understanding' question.

4. The food was tasty (1).
    AND/OR
    The fries were crisp (1).
    AND/OR
    The milkshakes were thick (1).

    > **TOP EXAM TIP**
    >
    > Some pupils find it helpful to underline key words in the questions to help them to focus on what is being looked for. In this question, the key word is 'popular'. Did you find this word in the third sentence of paragraph two? This time, the answer comes BEFORE the key word 'popular'. Remember that the answer can come before or after a key word or phrase so look <u>around</u> for the answer.
    >
    > You gain one mark for each reason you give for why McDonald's was popular – up to a maximum of two marks. There are three suggestions here but in your answer you only need to give two reasons to gain two marks.

5. Most men of his age would not want to start a new business/would want to retire/work less hard (1) and would not want to start a business/build a new company (1)

    > **HINT**
    >
    > You will often be asked about an idea in the passage but you have to answer 'in your own words'. Many pupils answer these questions by quoting the exact words from the passage. You will not be given any marks for doing this! For example, if you had written for this answer 'slowing down' without explaining what it means you would be given no marks as you have simply copied this phrase from the passage.

6. (a) 'rinky-dink' = poor quality/amateurish/not efficient or professional (2)
    (b) 'streamlined' (2)
        OR
        'efficient' (2)

    > **HINT**
    >
    > Did you notice that you can gain either two marks or 0 marks for your answers here? You are given two marks here if you get the answer right as Question 6A and 6B are quite difficult questions!

7. (a) They were on the cover of a magazine (1)
    (b) People visited often to see why the business was so successful (1)

    > **TOP EXAM TIP**
    >
    > Did you spot the word 'legendary' in the first sentence of paragraph 2? 'Legendary' means famous and examples of this are written in the next sentence.
    >
    > In question 4, you were asked to explain **in your own words** so there was no need to quote. And sometimes you are asked to **quote** so there is no need to use your own words. In question 7, you are not told to answer in your own words. So it is OK to use your own words OR quote.
    >
    > If you are ever not sure whether to quote or use your own words, do both!

8. He might want to take the credit/he wanted people to think he had discovered or invented McDonalds/he was the reason for its success (2).

> ### TOP EXAM TIP
>
> This question asks for your opinion – the key phrase in the question is 'Why do you think...'.
>
> Of course, your answer must be based on your understanding of the passage – as well as your general knowledge. In this case, you can work out from the passage that McDonalds was very successful and so you could guess that Ray Kroc might want to think this was all down to him.

9. (a) 'Metaphor' OR 'imagery' (1). It tells you that they announced/told/stated the numbers loudly (1).

   (b) They put up signs (1) saying how many they sold (1).

> ### TOP EXAM TIP
>
> This is an 'analysis' question which asks you about the writer's word choice. Did you spot that 'trumpeted' is a metaphor? Sometimes you will be told that you are analysing a metaphor or simile but – more likely - you will be asked to identify the technique just as you are in this question. Of course, you have to spot that this is an image and you should also know what type of image it is - a metaphor!

10. 1952: First franchise in Phoenix (1)
    1954: Ray Kroc arrived (1)

> ### TOP EXAM TIP
>
> In this question, the examiner helps you by telling you where to look for the answer! Just find the date 1952 and work out what happened then – the answer comes before the date. Then you are told that this was 'two years before' Ray Kroc arrived.

11. 'true heroes' (1)
    'remarkable men' (1)

12. (a) Customers would come to a window (1) rather than having items brought to the car (1).

    (b) They made the menu smaller/they put only seven things on the menu/they 'cut the menu to just seven items' (1).
    AND/OR
    They decided/chose what to give customers instead of customers deciding (1).
    AND/OR
    The burgers were smaller and cheaper (1).

    (c) 'novel' or' entirely novel' ('new' = no marks) (2)

13. Dashes are used to show that this phrase explains in more detail/adds extra information about the hamburger size (2)

TOP EXAM TIP

This is an 'analysis' question. In other words, you are being asked about the language the writer has used – HOW the writer writes. Any question that asks you about punctuation is an 'analysis' question.

HINT

You can learn how to answer 'punctuation' questions quite easily by knowing about the uses of various punctuation marks – here are some examples.

Commas – to separate items in a list, clarify sentences that could be misleading and/or used in direct speech

Semi-colon – to join two or more closely related ideas and/or to separate sets of items in a list when there are commas within the sets or lists

Colon or dash – to introduce a list or quotations and/or expand on the meaning of a previous idea

Two dashes – to separate out a phrase or clause or comment

Brackets – to separate a piece of additional information

14. The word 'flop' is informal/slang (1). It means the change was a complete/utter failure. (1)

TOP EXAM TIP

This is another 'analysis' question which asks you to think about the writer's craft. You are being asked about the words the writer has chosen to use.

When answering analysis questions, many pupils fall into the trap of explaining WHAT the sentence means. Of course, this sentence tells you that the change was not successful or was a failure or did not appeal to people. But the question asks you what is unusual or interesting about the word 'flop'– not what it means!

The question also asks you to say if the word choice is effective – it is effective because 'flop' does not just mean 'failure' but 'utter and complete failure'. This makes clear to us that the change was completely unsuccessful.

15. They appealed to families (1)
because they sold items for children such as fries and milkshakes (1).
OR
because the food tasted great (1).
OR
because it was cheap to feed a whole family (1).

TOP EXAM TIP

Did you know that 'clientele' means 'customers'? If so, then this question is straightforward as the word 'family' comes straight after it. Try to keep building your vocabulary in the run up to the exam by reading as much as possible and learning the meanings of any unfamiliar words – a large vocabulary will help you in the exam.

16. They invented machines and systems such as dispensers (1).

AND/OR

They introduced 'specialisation' where one person does one task (1).

AND/OR

Food was ready prepared so customers did not have to wait (1).

17. (*a*) I think McDonald's customers enjoyed eating at McDonald's (1) because they could collect their food from a window (1).

AND/OR

because the food was cheap and arrived quickly (1).

AND/OR

because you would have the same experience every time (1).

TOP EXAM TIP

You gain one mark for your opinion – either writing you think customers would enjoy eating at McDonald's or that they would not enjoy eating at McDonald's? There is no right or wrong answer here because this is your own opinion. Then you have to find reasons for your opinion from the passage to gain the second mark. There are three examples of reasons given above – you gain one mark for one reason.

(*b*) I think McDonald's employees enjoyed working at McDonald's. (1) They did not have to serve customers in their cars and they could concentrate on one task at a time (1).

OR

They used machines which made their jobs easier (1).

OR

They could prepare the food in advance (1).

OR

They only had to serve a small number of items (1).

TOP EXAM TIP

You gain one mark for your opinion – either writing you think employees would enjoy working at McDonald's or that they would not enjoy working at McDonald's? There is no right or wrong answer here because this is your own opinion. Then you have to find reasons for this from the passage. There are lots of examples of reasons given above.

18. C because Bill Bryson uses many facts and figures OR statistics about how it started OR who started it and what it sells. (2)

HINT

In question 18, you will gain one mark for identifying the purpose correctly and one mark for giving a clearly explained reason for your answer.

TOP EXAM TIP

You may be asked about purpose at General level. Think about why the writer has written the passage. Writers write texts for many different purposes. Look at the list of purposes below, and remember that a writer usually has one than one purpose.

- To entertain
- To inform
- To persuade
- To argue
- To explain
- To evaluate

19. The title is appropriate (1) because
    It contains information about McDonald's in the 1950s (1).
    OR
    It describes the development of McDonald's from 1950 onwards (1).
    OR
    It is about developments in technology (1).

TOP EXAM TIP

You are asked here for your opinion. You might think the title is not appropriate – as long as you give a clear, well-explained reason, you will get the marks. One mark is awarded for giving your opinion and the second mark is awarded for giving a reason for your opinion.

| PRACTICE EXAM C | CREDIT LEVEL WORKED ANSWERS |

1. (a) He visits to be given money (2)

   (b) 'familiar' (1)
       AND/OR
       'habit' (1)
       AND/OR
       'customary (1)
       AND/OR
       'always did' (1)
       AND/OR
       'as usual' (1)

TOP EXAM TIP

These questions ask you fairly straightforward information from the passage – why and how often the man visits John Pilger. In question 1, the answer you are looking for comes from paragraph 2 – 'money passed between us' – so remember that the answer could be anywhere near the beginning of the passage and is not always in the first or second sentence.

You are asked for two quotes in question 1b. Again, the answer could come from anywhere in paragraphs 1 or 2.

HINT | The first question is usually not the most difficult – this is because examiner wants you to feel confident from the word go. It will usually be an 'understanding' question – in other words, it will ask about an idea or ideas from the beginning of the passage and will test your general understanding.

2. (*a*) In return for the money (2)

AND/OR

To thank John Pilger for the money (2)

AND/OR

So the man can earn the money rather than be given the money for nothing (2)

TOP EXAM TIP

This is an evaluation question because it asks for your opinion – the key phrase in the question is 'Why do you think...?'

Of course, your answer must be based on your understanding of the passage – as well as your general knowledge. In this case, you can probably work out that the man is trying to repay John Pilger in some way as he offers to trim the hedge immediately after he has been handed the money. Three suggested wordings are given of the correct answer – you may have phrased your answer slightly differently.

(*b*) The writer thinks the man is not physically able OR unstable OR not firm OR too shaky OR too drunk to cut the hedge. (2)

HINT — Many pupils are unsure about where to find an answer. It can sometimes help to find a key word or phrase in the question (some pupils find highlighters useful to highlight these key words or phrases in the question). In the question, a key word is 'refuse'. So it can help to look for words which mean 'refuse' in the passage – in this case, 'I thanked him and said no...' The answer comes right after this phrase.

TOP EXAM TIP

This question asks you to explain 'too unsteady' in your own words.

At Credit level, you will often be asked about an idea in the passage but you have to answer 'in your own words'. Many pupils answer these questions by quoting the exact words from the passage. You will not be given any marks for doing this! The trick is to explain the word or phrase from the passage in your own way – this is called 'paraphrasing'.

3. Women move quickly away (1) and other people pretend he is not there/ignore him/are scared of him (1)

TOP EXAM TIP

If you use the technique of highlighting the key phrases in the question, here you would highlight 'other people' and 'react'. Then you would look in the passage to find mentions of these people and how they respond to the man. The examiner has helped you in this question by telling you where to look for the answer.

4. He agrees with how they behave OR he sympathises with them. (2).

HINT — Did you notice that you did not have to make two points in your answer this time – even though the question is worth two marks? Sometimes, examiners give two marks for an answer to a difficult question. This can make it tricky sometimes to work out how much to write!

If you do not give the correct answer you will be given 0 marks. (You will not be given any marks if you use the word 'understand' in your answer, for example, 'The writer understands how people feel' – can you work out why?)

TOP EXAM TIP

This question asks you about the writer's attitude – sometimes called the writer's 'stance'. You can work out the writer's stance from the words and ideas the writer uses. In the question, you are given the word 'understandably'. The writer is telling us that he understands or agrees with or sympathises with the situation other people are in when they come across 'the man with no name'.

Here are some other examples of words writers use to show their point of view:

- 'surprisingly'
- 'obviously'
- 'perhaps'
- 'possibly'
- 'suggest'
- 'unfortunately'
- 'hopefully'
- 'agree'

5. (a) 'where sick and alcoholic men go' (1)

   (b) 'where there was a murder' (1)

HINT

Most words have connotations. A connotation is a secondary meaning. For example, the primary meaning of 'home' is a 'residence' or 'dwelling place'. We all have different connotations or secondary meanings for the word 'home'. What does it mean to you? Perhaps it is a place of security or warmth? These are the connotations the word 'home' has for you. Connotations can be positive or negative. In this question, you are being asked about phrases that have negative or 'unpleasant' connotations.

TOP EXAM TIP

The word 'convey' simply means to communicate or to show to the reader. So the question is asking which phrases 'tell' you the idea of unpleasantness.

6. (a) Inverted commas are used as this is a direct quote from the newspaper advert (2).
   OR
   These are the actual words used in the newspaper advert. (2).

   (b) Inverted commas are used to show the writer does not think the hostels can be described as proper or real hotels.
   OR (2)
   Inverted commas are used to show the writer does not think the residents are treated as proper or real guests (2).

HINT

Do you know why writer use inverted commas (sometimes called quotations marks)? You should know these uses and be able to spot them.
Writers use inverted commas

- to show that the word(s) are being quoted

- to show that the writer is using a word(s) but with a different meaning

- to show that the writer is being ironic or sarcastic (by using the word but meaning the opposite!)

- to show speech, e.g. in fiction writing.

TOP EXAM TIP

You are very likely to be asked a punctuation question in a Credit exam. You can learn how to answer these questions quite easily by knowing about the uses of various punctuation marks – here are some examples.

- Commas – to separate items in a list, clarify sentences that could be misleading and/or used in direct speech
- Semi-colon – to join two or more closely related ideas and/or to separate sets of items in a list when there are commas within the sets or lists
- Colon or dash – to introduce a list or quotations and/or expand on the meaning of a previous idea
- Two dashes – to separate out a phrase or clause or comment
- Brackets – to separate a piece of additional information

7. (*a*) 'the true figure is greater' (2)

HINT This time, you are asked to quote directly from the passage. Always quote accurately – you are copying the writer's actual words so spell and punctuate these exactly as they are used.

TOP EXAM TIP

In question 3, you were told where to find the answer. Sometimes, you are not given this help and you have to read carefully for yourself. Always look for the key word or phrase in the question – using a highlighter can help with this. You might highlight '80,000' and 'not an accurate number' in this question. Then find these ideas in the passage and you will find the answer. Remember, though, that the answer could be found before the key word or phrase or after it. So always look <u>around</u> the word or phrase (this is called the 'direct context'). In this case, the answer is in the second sentence in the paragraph.

(*b*) The actual number (1) of homeless people is higher (1)

HINT Always 'have a go' at a question. You may feel you have no clue about the answer but if you write nothing, you will gain no marks! If you write an answer, you just might be correct so never leave an answer blank.

8. Christmas is a happy time when people may feel sympathy towards less fortunate people. (2)
OR
People may be sympathetic towards homeless people particularly when there is bad weather. (2)

TOP EXAM TIP

The key phrase in this 'evaluation' question is 'in your opinion'. In question 2, the key phrase in the question was 'Why do you think..?' Of course, you are being asked about a quotation from the passage so you have to focus on this but you can use your own general knowledge to help you answer.

9. (a) scared of the dark (1)
   AND/OR
   unsure where he would sleep (1)
   AND/OR
   more dangerous at night (1)
   AND/OR
   worries about what might happen (1)

   (b) scared/worried/frightened (1) about the weather/ wind/fire/his environment (1)

10. 'Furtiveness' (1) which means that the homeless person may be secretive/feel uncomfortable (1)
    OR
    'a sporadic, shallow joviality' (1) which means that the homeless person may occasionally seem happy (1)
    OR
    'a deferential way' (1) which means that the homeless person may act as though/ pretend he or she is less important /has fewer rights than other people/subservient/ obedient (1)

11. The man answers with emotional (1) exclamations (1)
    OR
    The man answers with exaggerated (1) exclamations (1)

TOP EXAM TIP

Melodramatic language is over-emotional, exaggerated language. Always remember the advice to 'have a go' at a question. Even if you did not know the meaning of melodramatic, you could have a guess based on what the man says.

---

12. This is an informal or colloquial or conversational phrase.

TOP EXAM TIP

It is important to be able to tell the difference between formal and informal language. Informal (sometimes called 'colloquial' or 'conversational') language is everyday, slangy language, for example, the kind of words you use in the playground or with your friends. Formal language is used for writing and when you are in a formal situation, e.g. a job interview, writing a school essay etc.

Formal	Informal
No slang	Slang
Fewer or no abbreviations	Abbreviations (e.g. 'isn't instead of 'is not')
Complex sentences	Simple sentences
Complex words	Simple words

TOP EXAM TIP: CREDIT

Both questions 11 and 12 ask you about the writer's word choice. You will always be asked about a writer's style at Credit level. The best practice is to read, read and read some more. This way, you will learn about how writers create effects through the words they use.

---

13. The writer is using the word 'wonderful' sarcastically (1) because he feels the opposite/that the expression is not wonderful (1).

> **HINT**
>
> Do you know the saying 'tone of voice'? This refers to the intonation someone uses when he or she speaks. It is very easy to spot when someone is being sarcastic or sympathetic through what they say and how they say it. It is much more difficult to spot the tone in a piece of writing. (If you find working out the tone difficult, try reading the text out loud – in your head!). A writer can be sarcastic, loving, arrogant, funny... Work this out from the words that he or she uses and always remember to quote the words or phrases in your answer.

14. 'Prey' is effective (1) as the man may be a victim of others more powerful than him (1)

OR

'Prey' is effective (1) as the man may feel he is being hunted or attacked by criminals or the police (1)

OR

'Prey' is effective (1) as the man may feel as if he is a defenceless animal (1)

> **TOP EXAM TIP: CREDIT**
>
> You are very likely to be asked about imagery in a Credit passage (these can also be called 'figures of speech' or 'metaphorical language'). Sometimes you will be told that you are analysing a metaphor or simile but – more likely – you may be asked to identify the type of image just as you are in this question.
>
> This question also asks for your evaluation of the effectiveness of the writer's word choice. In your answer, you could write that you find this an ineffective metaphor – as long as you give clear reasons why you do not find it effective!

15. This refers to the Government claim that it has reduced homelessness in the previous paragraph. (1) The function of the sentence is to disagree with or contradict this claim. (1)

> **TOP EXAM TIP**
>
> For one mark here, you have to refer to the word 'this'. For a second mark, you must explain that 'this' refers to the Government claim in the previous paragraph that it has reduced homelessness.

> **TOP EXAM TIP : CREDIT**
>
> You may be asked at Credit level to explain the function of a word, phrase or sentence. For example, you could be asked about the function of a sentence at the beginning or at the end of a paragraph, sometimes called a topic sentence.
>
> Often, the function of a sentence is to link – either with ideas before it or after it. There is usually a key word or phrase which 'signals' the function to you. In this question, there is no 'signal' word. You simply have to understand that 'this' refers back to the claim referred to previously.
>
> The function of a word or phrase can be to 'signal' added information, a summary, an explanation, to show a result, to contrast.
>
> Look at the linking words and phrases below – can you work out their functions?
>
> - *in short*
> - *furthermore*
> - *the former ... the latter ...*
> - *besides*
> - *since*
> - *as a result*
> - *nonetheless*
> - *unlike*

16. Tourists treat homeless people as similar to a tourist attraction/something to be looked at/visited (1). This is shown by the phrase a 'tourist curiosity'. (1)

OR

Tourists cannot believe (1) how many homeless people there are in London. This is shown by the word 'incredulous'. (1)

TOP EXAM TIP: CREDIT

Pupils often ask if answers should be written out in full sentences. It is always a good idea to write 'proper' sentences as so many of the questions ask you to 'explain'. Your ability to write clearly and explain fully is crucial – try to get into the habit of writing answers in full sentences unless the question specifically asks for a word or phrase only.

Use the amount of space provided as a guide to how much you should write.

---

17. (*a*) They cannot believe how many homeless people there are (1)
'incredulous' (1)

OR

They are very interested/want to know about the homeless (1)
'tourist curiosity' (1)

(*b*) The tour guide refers to homeless people as though they are rubbish/not human/do not have dignity or rights/something to be got rid of/something which needs to be cleaned away (1) – 'they were hosed away'.

18. The title is appropriate as the man is not named and is therefore anonymous. The writer's main argument is that there are large numbers of homeless people in the UK. The title therefore emphasises that homeless people may lose their sense of identity. (2)

19. John Pilger obviously disapproves of what the Government is doing to solve the problem of homelessness.

His argument is persuasive because he uses many examples to back up what he claims, for instance, he gives facts and figures about homeless people

OR

He uses his personal experience to describe 'the man with no name' which also makes his argument stronger.

OR

John Pilger uses emotive language such as 'suffering' and 'prey' which is persuasive. (2)

TOP EXAM TIP

In questions 17 and 18, you are asked to evaluate the title and how convincing or persuasive you find this article. The answers given here are examples of how you might answer these questions. As always with evaluation questions, base your answer on the passage but include your own opinion. You could say that you do not think the title is appropriate – or that the article is unconvincing – as long as you can justify your answer with evidence from the passage.

You are given a clue to the writer's attitude in the introduction to the passage (this is called the 'rubric'). This information can be very useful so don't ignore it and plunge straight into the passage. It can often give you clues about the writer's audience and purpose so read it carefully.

In this case, the rubric tells you that the writer 'blames' homelessness on the Government so you can guess that he sympathises with homeless people and is critical of the Government.

INTRODUCTION

This section gives you advice about the Standard Grade English Writing exam. The first part gives you general help with how to write in the exam. The second part gives you specific advice about how to tackle each writing option.

As well as advice, you will find.

TOP EXAM TIP

These are 'at a glance' tasks to do or advice to remember

TOP EXAM TIP: CREDIT

These contain specific advice for pupils hoping to gain a Credit award

---

All pupils – whether working at Credit, General or Foundation level - sit the same Writing paper. The Writing paper is in booklet form and contains anything between 20 and 25 questions/essay titles. There are also pictures and photographs on the left hand side pages of the booklet. In the exam, you will choose ONE of the questions/ essay titles.

You are given 75 minutes for this exam. You should always spend some of this time planning what you are going to write. Take your time at this stage – it is better to spend 10 minutes calmly choosing and planning your writing than to start writing in a hurry, change your mind and have to start all over again!

Give yourself an hour for the actual writing itself – how many words can you write in an hour? If you do not know, you should find this out. We all write at different speeds so you can only find this out on your own. Your friends could be very fast or very slow writers so don't compare yourself with them. Work out how much you can write and aim to be able to do this in the exam itself.

If you often run out of time, practice will help. For example, you may be trying to write stories that are simply too long – perhaps because you do not spend time on planning the plot/storyline and so try to cover too much in the story itself. Practise planning and writing simpler shorter stories – fewer characters or fewer events perhaps – and this may help you to finish on time.

Always leave 5 minutes at the end for a final read through. Even if you have not finished your writing, try to take time for a check. Spelling and punctuation errors can spoil the overall effect of a piece of writing so take the time to ensure your sentences make sense.

TOP EXAM TIP

Every year, a number of pupils do not follow the instructions at the beginning of the paper which tell you to choose ONE question from the paper.

There are usually between 20 and 25 questions to choose from. Choose ONE only!

Preparation before the big day!

Lots of people will tell you that you can't prepare for the English Writing paper. The truth is that you <u>can</u> prepare for the Writing paper and the more preparation you do, the better your writing will be.

The best preparation is to write, write, write! Whether it is letters or emails to your friends, stories, your diary or writing for other subjects like History, all writing practice will be useful when it comes to the exam. Of course, you will not know exactly what Writing questions will be in the exam paper but you can practise by looking at past papers – or working through some examples from the Writing Paper in this book – because the same types of writing almost always appear in the exam. For example, there are usually questions that ask you to write short stories, to write about personal experience, descriptive writing and so on. So looking at practice papers will give you a very good idea of what to expect.

TOP EXAM TIP

The proper term for a type of writing is 'genre'. How many genres are there in English? Challenge yourself to see how many you can come up with!

Using pictures/photographs

Another good way to prepare for the exam is to look at photographs or pictures and use these pictures to help your writing. There are always pictures and/or photos in the Writing exam paper so this will be good practice for the exam day itself. Don't ignore the pictures in the paper. A photo or picture is there to help you. It can give you ideas and inspiration. Really look at the picture in detail and think of words and ideas as you examine it. For example, you might be shown a photo of a dark, gloomy forest and one of the tasks is to write an atmospheric piece of descriptive writing. As you look closely at the picture, you may think of words like 'frightening', 'secretive', 'silent'. You may even see a dim ruined castle in a corner of the picture and this might spark off an idea – perhaps you could include a description of the castle as well as the forest? Let your imagination run wild … Don't worry if you find it challenging to use pictures for inspiration – you do not have to use ideas from the photo or picture at all if you do not want to. And there are always questions at the end of the paper without any pictures.

Choosing a genre

Another good idea is to practise more than one type of writing. You may love writing short stories and so you may have decided to write one in the exam. But what if the short story questions in the exam do not appeal to you? Practise writing at least TWO genres to prepare for the exam. For example, you may enjoy writing informative pieces such as news articles or reports but you could also practise your personal writing so you have more questions to choose from in the exam.

TOP EXAM TIP

Don't forget about spelling, punctuation and paragraphing. A good way to work on these aspects is to get someone – a teacher, a friend, your parent/carer – to look over your work. Get into the habit of reading over your work by reading it out loud, in your head or to friends or family to make sure your writing makes sense.

On examination day

Firstly, punctuation, spelling and grammar. These are sometimes called the 'technical' aspects of English. All your sentences must make sense clearly 'at first reading'. This means the examiner should not have to re-read a sentence because the meaning is unclear. Place commas in the right places especially when you are writing complex sentences. Do try to write as accurately as you can. Checking over your work by reading it to yourself can help to ensure your sentences make sense. If it doesn't make sense to you, it won't make sense to the examiner!

> ## TOP EXAM TIP: CREDIT
>
> You can make a few errors in punctuation, spelling or grammar and still achieve a general award. However if you want to achieve a Credit grade, try to eliminate these. You sentence structure has to be accurate so practise writing long complex sentences with plenty of clauses. Read quality newspapers to find examples of interesting sentence structures.
> For a Grade 1, your paragraphs and sentences have to be 'skillful'.

Now, length. Pupils often ask how long an essay written in an exam has to be. The simple answer is that there is no limit because we all write at different speeds and we all write different amounts. Also, think about your purpose. You might choose to write 'in any way' about a given title and you choose to write a poem. A poem of, say, 600–700 words would be very long indeed! This is what is meant by the phrase 'appropriate to purpose'. The length should 'fit' the purpose – and of course is also related to the amount of time you have in the exam.

Let's think some more about this idea of purpose. You must be very clear about the purpose of the writing task you choose. For example, you might choose to write a short story. One of the main purposes of a short story is to entertain the reader. So your story has to be entertaining! If your purpose is to create a gently humorous story that will make the reader laugh, then it must communicate this gentle humour. Otherwise, it won't 'fulfil its purpose'. Never change purpose in the middle of a piece of writing – if you start writing a short story about a character in a dilemma, don't get carried away so much that this turns into a personal story about a time when you were in a dilemma. You can, of course, think about your own experience and even use some of these details, but you must stick to the purpose in the question.

Words, words, words …

What about the actual words you use? When writing, pupils can sometimes be so busy with character, setting, ideas, organisation and all the rest that they forget about the actual words they are using! Try to use language in interesting and original ways – not just as words to tell a story or explain an experience or express an opinion.

You could use:

- imagery such as similes and metaphors
- interesting sentence structures – different sentence lengths and patterns
- language to create a mood or atmosphere, for example to build up tension in a ghost story

Have a look at the Practice Close Reading passages. The writers of these passages have all used interesting and original language.

TOP EXAM TIP: CREDIT

For a Credit award, you have to use accurate vocabulary and you have to use a variety of words. Extend your vocabulary by reading as much as you can – and keep a dictionary beside you, so that when you come across a word you don't know, you can look it up and store it away for your own use. Reading quality newspapers will also help.

PERSONAL WRITING

1. Write about a journey or trip you have made. Remember to include your thoughts and feelings.
4. Write about your experience of a new baby in the family. Remember to include your thoughts and feelings.
8. Write about your hopes and dreams for the future.
15. Write about the music you enjoy and what it means to you.
21. 'It wasn't us!' Write about an experience you have had where you were part of a group blamed for something.

These questions are all examples of Personal Writing. The important thing to remember – whether you are writing about something that has already happened (for example, question 1) or about things which might happen in the future (for example, question 10) – is to write 'from the heart'. The best Personal Writing is truthful and open and describes your feelings and emotions clearly. For example, if you do not play tennis, it would be difficult to pretend you know all about tennis and to write honestly about how it makes you feel.

Remember also that Personal Writing should include description of sights, sounds, surroundings, atmosphere – if you do not include this kind of description, your writing will end up being a list of events and nothing else. Try to make your writing lively and not just 'Then we did this', or 'Then I did that'! This is one reason why the question usually reminds you to include your 'thoughts and feelings'.

Can you spot the differences between the two extracts below?

We got up at 5 o'clock in the morning. We were very tired. We packed our cases and waited for the taxi. The taxi arrived and we went to the airport.

We got up at 5 o'clock in the morning and looked out of the frosty icy window. We were very tired but so excited to be heading off towards heat and sunshine! We packed our cases, the two of us sitting on them to make sure they closed. They sprang open every time we tried to stuff in another last minute 'essential'. The taxi arrived promptly at 6 o'clock and whisked us off to the airport.

This type of writing is about your emotions. It is about reflecting on how you felt or feel about something or someone. When you are writing about an experience, you should explain how you felt before, during and after the experience. For example, if you choose Question 21, describe your feelings/emotions:
- before the event (before you were blamed)
- at the time of/during the event (the moment when you were blamed)
- afterwards (when the true culprit was found).

This is called 'chronological order' – in other words, write about the events you are describing in the order that they happened. So, if you choose question 5 about a new baby in the family, you could use the chronological order below

- When/how I found out mum was expecting
- My feelings when I found out
- First six months – mum very well, my exams!
- Last three months – mum in hospital, baby early
- Birth – what happened/my feelings
- How I feel now baby is 12 months old

It is more difficult to choose a structure if you are writing questions 4, 8 or 15. This is because these ask you about the future or about something which is not a 'one-off' event. Your essay should have a clear structure so think about how you will organise your writing. For example, in question 15, you could use the structure below:

- Introduction
- How/when/why I started playing the trumpet
- My band
- How I have improved – my teacher/practice
- Competitions/prizes I have won
- My dreams of playing at the Albert Hall

In question 10, you will have to think about how you want to organise your writing. Perhaps you could divide your hopes and dreams into different areas – your career ambitions, your hopes about your family, your interests, your dream of becoming rich and famous! So your writing will have four main sections.

Some pupils find mind maps helpful to organise their writing. Here is a mind map of the ideas for question 10:

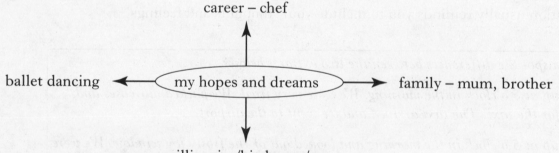

For question 4, how about writing first about where you want to be, your goal? Then write about the different ways you are going to reach or have reached this goal, finishing off with the importance of achieving your goal at the end?

Remember that you can organise your Personal Writing in any way that 'fits' with what you are writing about – as long as it is organised!

Personal Writing is a very popular choice for many pupils. It is a chance to write about yourself and about something that has happened to you so, because everyone is different no-one will be able to write exactly the same as you. A lot of pupils choose this option so try to make your writing stand out. If you follow the advice above, you will be well on the way to writing success.

TOP EXAM TIP: CREDIT

For a Credit award, you have to show 'insight and self-awareness' in your personal writing – so write about an experience that you have reflected on in depth and that has helped you learn things about yourself. You also have to express your feelings and reactions with 'sensitivity'. This means being able to understand and explain your emotions, showing you are aware of why you have acted or reacted in a certain way.

SHORT STORY

2. Write a short story about a character who makes a train journey. You should develop setting, character and plot.

7. Write a short story using the following opening
    He emerged from the time machine and looked out over a strange crystal city he did not recognise. The buildings shone brightly but there was no movement. No life.

12. Write a short story about a sporting champion who loses a match/game at a crucial time. You should develop setting, character and plot.

14. Write a short story about a busker. You should develop setting, character and plot.

20 Write a short story in which the main character makes a life-changing decision. You should develop setting and character as well as plot.

Usually, a 'short story' question will help you with what you need to do – you will be told 'You should develop setting and character as well as plot'. So that is exactly what you should do!

Many pupils write short stories that have lots of action happening (the 'plot' or 'storyline') but they forget to develop the setting of the story or the character(s).

Setting

TOP EXAM TIP

Describe the setting – both time and place. This can be done in 'chunks', for example, in a paragraph(s) near the beginning of your writing and/or can be 'spread' throughout your writing.

Here is an example of description of setting (place) from the beginning of a story:

The birthday cake lay trampled on the kitchen floor, candles and tiny bits of icing and sugar scattered over the table. The kitchen was ruined, chairs upset and cutlery, plates, cups all dirty and torn. Missy stood in the centre of the room, sobbing quietly.

Here is an example of a description of setting (time) from the beginning of a story:

It was the end of the war. Richard sighed as took off his khaki army uniform with its tight jacket and brass buttons and counted out his few remaining shillings. Time to go home.

Can you spot 'clues' to where and when these stories take place?

Characters

One very common mistake pupils make is to assume that the reader knows all about a character. Remember that although you may feel you know a character, you need to describe him or her to the reader in using plenty of detail.

So make sure you develop your character(s) – ask yourself:

- How does she/he change, develop, grow?
- How does he/she behave and speak?
- What does he/she look like?
- How does he/she relate to other people?
- What are his/her opinions/point of view?

Show what characters are like through the way they speak, act and through their relationships.

Theme

What will the theme of your story be? Sometimes, the question will tell you this – for example, in Question 20, you are told that a 'life change' will be the theme of this story – but how will you develop this theme? Will the life change be a positive decision for all the characters? What are the results of the life change? How will the story end? Will your story have a moral or message such as 'Don't cry over spilt milk'?

TOP EXAM TIP

Popular themes include:

- Relationships
- Conflict
- Love
- Good versus evil
- Freedom

Can you think of any others you would like to write about?

TOP EXAM TIP: CREDIT

For a Grade 1 or 2, you should show you are skilled in all the aspects of fiction writing above - creating and developing character, describing setting ... and it goes without saying that examiners are looking for great imagination in Credit writing!

Whatever grade you are aiming to achieve, you will have to organise your story. It needs to have a beginning, a middle and an end. Usually, a story will build towards a climax towards the end of the story. For example, if you are answering question 20, the 'life-changing decision' could happen about two-thirds of the way through the story – after you have built up your plot and developed your characters. After your character makes the decision, you could write about the effects of this.

You can use techniques such as flashbacks to create a more interesting structure. The important thing is to plan out the structure before you start. That way, your story won't 'ramble' and the reader will be able to follow the plot clearly.

Short stories are always very popular with pupils – so try to make yours stand out from the crowd.

DISCURSIVE WRITING

> 5. Over 9000 babies are born each year in Scotland to mothers aged between 13 and 19. Give your views.
>
> 9. Mobile phones – a nuisance or an essential piece of technology? Give your views.
>
> 13. The Scottish Government wants to encourage school pupils to be healthy, for example, by providing healthy school dinners and encouraging pupils to take PE. Give your views.
>
> 16. 'Pop is actually my least favourite kind of music because it lacks real depth.' (Christina Aguilera) Give your views.
>
> 17. Zoos are cruel and inhumane. Give your views.

This type of writing should not be attempted unless you have thought about the subject before the exam! If you have never reflected on zoos and zoo conditions, have never visited a zoo and don't really like animals, you are not going to write a convincing essay about why you think such places are cruel.

You should try to include facts and information in Discursive Writing and you will only have these if you have read or thought about the topic in advance. For example, if you are writing about mobile phones, do you know how many people own a mobile phone, statistics about mobile phone companies, information about the alleged dangers to your health of using mobile phones? Background knowledge always improves Discursive Writing because it shows you are knowledgeable about the topic and have already thought about it.

If you choose to write a Discursive essay, you should be very organised because a clear structure is a requirement of this type of writing.

The first thing to do is to decide what you think about the topic. Do you agree, disagree or can you 'see' both sides of the argument? You should state your opinion about this clearly at the beginning of your essay. This will be your introductory paragraph.

You should then explain the arguments for or against (or both) in the main body of the essay. The way to organise this clearly is to use topic sentences. A topic sentence is usually the first sentence in a paragraph, although it can actually occur anywhere in the paragraph. (Why not try experimenting with writing a paragraph and placing the topic sentences in different places within the paragraph?) The topic sentence explains the main point you make in the paragraph, for example, you think zoos are cruel because all the animals are caged or locked in. Remember that you should include information and examples in each paragraph too.

Your conclusion should repeat your opinion clearly and 'finish off' your essay strongly.

TOP EXAM TIP

It's important to stick to your opinion – don't change your mind halfway through! You either agree, disagree or you can understand both sides. Make sure the end of your essay 'matches' the beginning.

TOP EXAM TIP: CREDIT

To improve on your Discursive skills – and hopefully be awarded a top grade – ensure that your ideas are complex and that you organise your ideas and arguments very clearly.

You also need to:

- be objective; show you can 'stand back' from the topic, for example, by showing understanding of others' opinions
- generalise; show you can make general statements as well as using specific examples
- evaluate; show you can make a judgement about your own and others' points of view

There is a lot of advice about Discursive Writing in Leckie & Leckie's *Standard Grade Revision Notes*. Have a look at this for plenty of useful advice: see www.leckieandleckie.co.uk

WRITING IN A SPECIFIC FORMAT

Questions 3 and 11 ask you to write a letter. If you choose this question, you must be familiar with the correct layout for a letter – in both questions, you are being asked to write a formal letter.

Can you remember all the rules about the layout and language in this type of letter?

- Where should your address should go?
- Where should you add the date?
- Should you include the address you are writing to?
- How should you start the letter?
- What do you call the person you are writing to?
- Should you use paragraphs?
- How do you finish off the letter?

If you are unclear about this, give this question a miss!

Letters also need to have a clear structure – look at the suggested structure below for a letter of complaint:

Introduction – state clearly the issue you wish to write/complain about.

      Explain your opinion about it.

      Give some facts and figures which support your opinion.

Middle section – explain in more detail about the problem.

      Give examples of what this means/has meant for you/your community.

Conclusion – restate your opinion.

      Explain what you want to be done about the situation. (For example, you could make positive suggestions about alternatives.)

There are occasionally questions that ask you to write in other formats, for example, a newspaper article or a speech or a diary or a play script. There is not enough space here for advice on all these types. However, you should attempt this type of question only if you are very familiar with the format, layout and language that you should use.

DESCRIPTIVE WRITING

> 19. Describe the scene brought to mind by one of the following:
>   'A full moon hangs, a round, white blaze.'
>   OR
>   'Bare branches in winter are a form of writing.'

This is one of the most challenging types of writing – but if you are a confident writer with a very well – developed vocabulary, it could be the one for you.

- Do you love using imagery and description using plenty of adjectives in original ways?
- Are you able to describe a person, an object, a landscape for longer than a few paragraphs?
- Are you able to organise your descriptive writing? For example, you might decide to describe each aspect of the scene in turn and so you will have to decide on an order for this.

TOP EXAM TIP

Try to appeal to all five senses in descriptive writing – not just what you can see in the scene.

- What can be heard?
- What textures are there?
- What can be touched or felt?
- What can be smelt?
- What can be tasted?

You don't have to describe all five senses but even using one or two will make your writing livelier and more interesting.

Think about how to narrate your writing –

'I watch the moon slip down...'

OR

'The moon slips down...'

Which do you prefer?

If you enjoy Descriptive Writing, it can be tempting to write randomly all sorts of great descriptive words and phrases just as they come to you! But a descriptive essay needs to have some kind of logical order so that the reader can follow it clearly.

Could you

- use the five senses as five 'sections' in your essay?
- describe each aspect of the scene in turn, e.g. trees, branches, twigs, sky?
- describe the scene from different places, e.g. as though you are moving through the scene, e.g. watching the moon from ground level, halfway up a hill, at the top of the hill?

TOP EXAM TIP

To improve your descriptive writing, look at photographs or pictures and practise describing these in as much detail as you can.

Remember that you have 75 minutes to write in the exam so you need to include as much detail as possible.

WRITE IN ANY WAY...

> 6. ' Bringing Up Baby.' Write in any way you like using this title
> 10. Write in any way you like about the picture above.
> 18. You've got a friend.' Write in any way you like about friendship.

These questions are great if you do not find a question in the paper that 'springs out' at you – or if you are good at lots of types of writing. These questions give you freedom to choose what genre you want to write. You could write a poem, a drama script, a fictional diary... just remember that you have to be confident and experienced in writing the genre you choose.

Of course, all the usual rules apply – planning your writing, organising it well with a clear structure, expressing yourself clearly and well – whatever you write.

TOP EXAM TIP: CREDIT

Whichever type of writing you choose in the exam, for a Credit grade, your ideas and/or information have to be well organised. On top of that, try to demonstrate to the examiner that you can 'select and highlight' what is most significant. Linking words and phrases can help with this as well as thinking about the order of your ideas.

Most importantly, enjoy yourself! There is lots to think about when you are creating a piece of writing, especially under exam pressure, but try to relax and enjoy the opportunity to let your imagination run free!